W9-CTD-528

ARCTIC OCEAN

ARCTIC OCEAN

ICELAND

NORWAY

FINLAND

SWEDEN

ESTONIA

R U S S I A

UNITED
KINGDOM

DENMARK

LATVIA
LITHUANIA

IRELAND

NETHERLANDS
BELGIUM
LUX.

POLAND

BELARUS

GERMANY
CZECH
REP.
SLOVAKIA

FRANCE

SWITZ.

AUSTRIA

HUNGARY

UKRAINE

MOLDOVA

KAZAKHSTAN

MONGOLIA

ANDORRA

SLOVENIA

ITALY

CROATIA

Bosnia-
Herz.

SERBIA
MONT.

ROMANIA

BULGARIA

MACED.

NORTH
KOREA

SOUTH
KOREA

JAPAN

PORTUGAL

SPAIN

ALBANIA

GREECE

GEORGIA

ARMENIA

TURKEY

AZER-
BAIJAN

UZBEKISTAN

KYRGYZSTAN

TAJIKISTAN

CHINA

MALTA

CYPRUS

SYRIA

LEBANON

TURKMENISTAN

MOROCCO

TUNISIA

ISRAEL

JORDAN

IRAQ

IRAN

AFGHANISTAN

TAIWAN

NORTH
PACIFIC
OCEAN

ALGERIA

LIBYA

EGYPT

KUWAIT
BAHRAIN

QATAR

SAUDI
ARABIA

U.A.E.

PAKISTAN

NEPAL

BHUTAN

INDIA

BANGLA-
DESH

CAPE
VERDE

MAURITANIA

MALI

NIGER

CHAD

SUDAN

ERITREA

YEMEN

OMAN

MYANMAR

LAOS

SENEGAL

GAMBIA

GUINEA-
BISSAU

GUINEA

SIERRA LEONE

BURKINA
FASO

CÔTE
D'IVOIRE

GHANA

NIGERIA

BENIN

TOGO

LIBERIA

CENTRAL
AFRICAN REP.

SOUTH
SUDAN

DJIBOUTI

ETHIOPIA

THAILAND

CAMBODIA

VIETNAM

PHILIPPINES

MARSHALL
ISLANDS

SÃO TOMÉ & PRÍNCIPE

EQUAT. GUINEA

CAMEROON

GABON

REP. OF THE CONGO

DEM. REP.
OF CONGO

UGANDA

RWANDA
BURUNDI

KENYA

SOMALIA

BRUNEI

MALAYSIA

SINGAPORE

PALAU

FEDERATED
STATES OF
MICRONESIA

NAURU

KIRIBATI

SRI LANKA

MALDIVES

I N D O N E S I A

PAPUA
NEW GUINEA

TANZANIA

SEYCHELLES

INDIAN
OCEAN

EAST TIMOR

SOLOMON
ISLANDS

TUVALU

SAMOA

ANGOLA

ZAMBIA

MALAWI

COMOROS

MADAGASCAR

MAURITIUS

VANUATU

FIJI

TONGA

NAMIBIA

ZIMBABWE

MOZAMBIQUE

BOTSWANA

NEW
CALEDONIA

SWAZILAND

SOUTH
ATLANTIC
OCEAN

SOUTH
AFRICA

LESOTHO

A U S T R A L I A

SOUTH
PACIFIC
OCEAN

NEW
ZEALAND

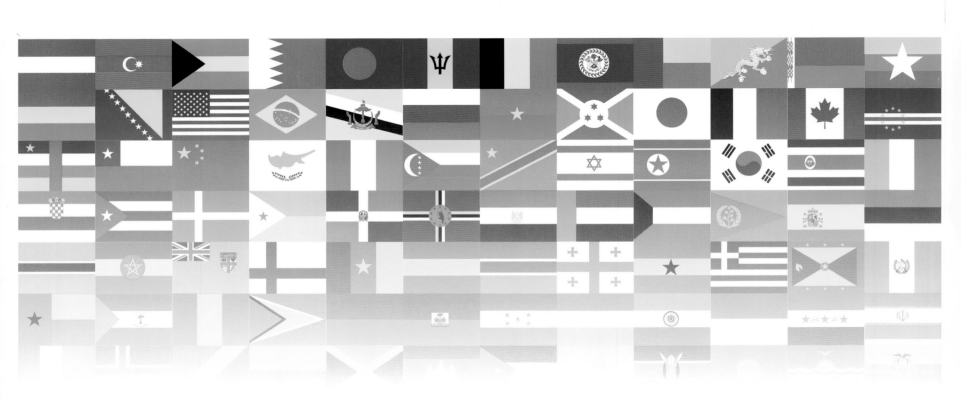

FLAGS
OF THE
WORLD

FLAGS
OF THE
WORLD

SYLVIE BEDNAR

Illustrations by Christelle Guénot and Anne Steinlein

Abrams Books for Young Readers, New York

INTRODUCTION

A flag can tell you a lot about its country. Flags represent the history, legends and beliefs, and sometimes even the geographic location of a country! Most flags are created when a country becomes independent, which makes them a symbol of the nation's freedom.

The origin of flags goes back to ancient times. For thousands of years, nations and tribes have used flags to symbolize their cultures and beliefs. The Roman Legion carried an early type of flag—called a *vexillum* in Latin—that gave its name to the scholarly study of flags, which is known as vexillology.

It wasn't until the widespread dissemination of silk in the sixth century (discovered in China two thousand years earlier) that the flag as we know it came to be. Made of fabric attached to a simple piece of bamboo, so light it seemed to float in air, this object marked the birth of the modern flag.

CONTENTS

EUROPE

DENMARK

Children from around the world are familiar with the story "The Little Mermaid," written by Danish writer Hans Christian Andersen. But how many of them know the legendary story of the Danish flag?

It goes back to the Middle Ages during the time of the Crusades—military expeditions waged against pagans to convert them to the Christian faith. Danish soldiers were suffering great losses, and it seemed as if a critical battle would be lost. Suddenly a great red cloth marked with a white cross fell from the sky. The crusaders hoisted it up as a banner and miraculously won the battle! While no one knows if the story is true, we do know that Denmark's is the world's oldest national flag, flown since 1625.

Continent: Europe
Capital: Copenhagen
Currency: Danish krone
Official language: Danish
Area: 16,640 sq. mi.
Highest point: Yding Skovhøj (568 ft.)

The Nordic Crusades were waged in the Middle Ages between Nordic Christians and the pagans from the Baltic Sea.

ICELAND Capital: Reykjavik

SWEDEN Capital: Stockholm

Together, these northern European countries form Scandinavia.

Finland's flag highlights the colors characteristic of the country: Blue symbolizes its 190,000 lakes, while white stands for the snow and white nights typical of a Finnish summer.

In **Iceland's** flag, the color red symbolizes volcanic eruptions of lava; white, the glaciers; and blue, the sky, sea, and waterfalls.

The **Swedish** flag features colors associated with traditional Swedish weapons, and is also reminiscent of the sky and sun—blue and gold.

In **Norway's** flag, the colors blue, white, and red represent democracy: These colors also appear on the flags of the United States, the United Kingdom, and France.

NORWAY Capital: Oslo

FINLAND Capital: Helsinki

RUSSIA

Bordered by the Baltic Sea to the west and the Pacific Ocean to the east, Russia extends along the length of the Arctic Ocean, spanning eleven time zones! In the seventeenth century, Czar Peter I (called Peter the Great because he was nearly six and a half feet tall) brought back the colors of the national flag from his travels in Europe. Captivated by the Dutch flag, he simply changed the order of the flag's rows when he returned to his native Russia. He also gave new meaning to the colors: White became the color of the czar; blue, the nobility; and red, the people.

This colorful harmony makes up the range of colors adopted by Pan-Slavic countries and has become a source of inspiration for a number of other flags throughout Eastern Europe.

Continent: Europe
Capital: Moscow
Currency: ruble
Official language: Russian
Area: 6,592,800 sq. mi.
Highest point: Mount Elbrus (18,510 ft.)

The hammer and the sickle, symbols of the Communist Party, appeared on the Russian flag between 1922 and 1991.

BELARUS

In this Eastern European country, flocks of children celebrate national holidays by proudly donning traditional dress: long white shirts and tunics adorned with embroidered red geometric shapes.

The same ornamental patterns are featured on the national flag, symbolizing the rich cultural heritage of Belarus.

As for the color choices, they correspond to the country's identity: The red stripe is reminiscent of the fact that Belarus was once Communist, as red is the symbolic color of this political ideology. The green stripe brings to mind the lush forests of the country, where bears and bison roam to this day.

Continent: Europe
Capital: Minsk
Currency: Belarusian ruble
Official languages: Belarusian, Russian
Area: 80,153 sq. mi.
Highest point: Mount Dzyarzhynskaya (1,135 ft.)

Traditional embroidery is entirely handmade, requiring hours of work and plenty of dexterity!

17

SLOVENIA

Slovenia's coat of arms depicts its geographical particularity: mountains! In it, you can see the three snow-covered peaks of the Alps' Mount Triglav, the highest point in the country. The undulating blue lines below it represent the rivers Sava and Drava.

What about the stars in the dark blue sky? They shine with all their might to symbolize three historic moments in the nation's history, including achieving independence. As for the white, red, and blue stripes, they represent Slovenia's place in the Slavic culture. These colors, known as the Pan-Slavic colors, are also found on the Russian flag.

Continent: Europe
Capital: Ljubljana
Currency: euro
Official language: Slovene
Area: 7,827 sq. mi.
Highest point: Mount Triglav (9,396 ft.)

Do brown bears frighten you? Then be careful, because Slovenia has plenty of them.

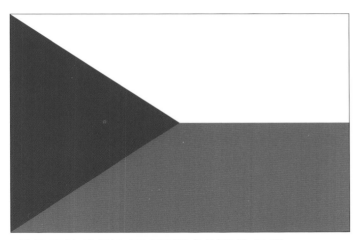

CZECH REPUBLIC

Capital: Prague

Blue, white, and red

These colors, which are also found on the Russian and Slovenian flags, are known as the **Pan-Slavic colors**: They symbolize a link to Slavic roots, history, and culture.

These colors were originally derived from the flag of the Russian Empire.

By following the example of Russia, the first Slavic country to have adopted this tricolored flag, these countries demonstrate that they share a common identity.

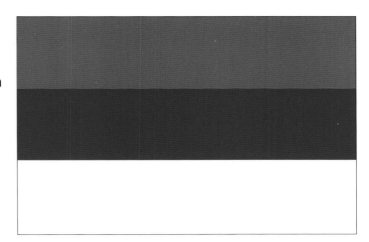

SERBIA Capital: Belgrade

CROATIA Capital: Zagreb

SLOVAKIA Capital: Bratislava

ESTONIA
Capital: Tallinn

The blue stripe of the Estonian flag evokes the Baltic Sea. Black represents the dark, marshy lands of this flat country. A blanket of white covers the land for nearly six months of the year, which, as you can see, is illustrated by a white stripe.

LITHUANIA
Capital: Vilnius

The yellow stripe of the Lithuanian flag evokes light and wheat fields, but yellow also represents the generosity and nobility of the people. Forests are represented by the green stripe, the color of life and liberty. And the red stripe symbolizes the blood spilled by this country's people while battling the Teuton, Russian, and German invaders.

UKRAINE
Capital: Kiev

The colors of the Ukrainian flag illustrate some of the country's natural elements: The blue and yellow horizontal stripes symbolize blue sky over the wheat of the steppes, as wheat is one of the country's primary sources of revenue. The colors also appear in the country's coat of arms, which depicts a golden lion on a blue field.

BULGARIA
Capital: Sofia

The Bulgarian flag uses green to represent natural riches. This country is world renowned for its vineyards and tobacco. Bulgaria is also the sixteenth-biggest grower of rice in the world. The white stripe stands for the Balkan mountain range, which crosses the eastern part of the country. But it especially symbolizes peace, cherished by an independent people who, for five centuries, were ruled by the Turks.

LATVIA

In 1180 the Latvians fought against the Teutonic knights, who were determined to convert the pagans to Christianity as part of the Nordic Crusades. According to legend, in order to rouse their courage for battle, Latvian soldiers assembled under immense tents stained with the juice of blackberries. Little by little, Latvian warriors began wearing this dark red color while fighting. So it is with great pride that Latvians today wave their red-white-red flag. The color white emphasizes the importance they attach to honor and truth.

Continent: Europe
Capital: Riga
Currency: lats
Official language: Latvian
Area: 24,938 sq. mi.
Highest point: Galzina Kalns (1,024 ft.)

When you pick blackberries, notice the fruit's dark red juice, the very color of the Latvian flag.

POLAND

Why did countries as different as Poland, Indonesia, and Monaco adopt the same colors for their flags? It's a mystery . . . but Poland, contrary to the other two, has white on top and red on the bottom. These colors are derived directly from the Polish royal coat of arms, which dates to the thirteenth century: a crowned eagle spreading its white wings against a red background. For the Poles, the eagle has always been a symbol of courage, strength, and majesty. The colors red and white are also a nod to Slavic identity, to which Poland belongs.

Continent: Europe
Capital: Warsaw
Currency: zloty
Official language: Polish
Area: 120,728 sq. mi.
Highest point: Mount Rysy (8,199 ft.)

The eagle serves as a symbol for a number of countries. Was it the bird's piercing stare and powerful claws that inspired them?

GERMANY

The three colored stripes of the German flag may never have come about if not for the crushing defeat of the army of the Napoleonic Empire by Prussian soldiers during the Battle of Nations at Leipzig in 1813.

In homage to the courageous and valiant soldiers who fought there, the Freikorps, the three colors of their uniforms—black, with red lapels and golden buttons (very flashy!)—were transformed into the horizontal stripes of the flag. It's a convenient way of remembering the flag of the most populous country in Europe!

Continent: Europe
Capital: Berlin
Currency: euro
Official language: German
Area: 137,856 sq. mi.
Highest point: Zugspitze (9,718 ft.)

The Freikorps of Baron von Lützow's army made quite a statement in their gold-buttoned uniforms.

BELGIUM

One could easily confuse the Belgian and German flags! How did these bordering countries' flags come to resemble each other so much? Did they copy each other? Not at all! The Belgian flag, which dates back to 1831, was inspired by the coat of arms of the family of the Duchy of Brabant, which depicted a golden lion against a black background, with sharp red claws and tongue. It was a clever way of scaring off intruders!

As for the resemblance between the German and Belgian flags, luckily the directions of the stripes are different.

Continent: Europe
Capital: Brussels
Currency: euro
Official languages: German, French, Dutch
Area: 11,787 sq. mi.
Highest point: Botrange (2,277 ft.)

The Duchy of Brabant adopted as its symbol the lion, known for its strength and power.

25

UNITED KINGDOM

This flag is so famous throughout the world that it even has a nickname— the Union Jack! It flies in the upper left corner of the Blue Ensign, the flag of the British merchant marine, and nowadays even appears on the covers of English rock music CDs: It's everywhere!

Do you know what all these diagonal colors symbolize? The Union Jack came about in 1606, three years after the union between the kingdoms of England, Scotland, and Wales. The flag's designers superimposed the white cross of Saint Andrew, patron saint of Scotland, over the red cross of Saint George, patron saint of England, over a blue background. Later on, the cross of Saint Patrick, patron saint of Ireland, was added to the flag. The only country of the United Kingdom not represented on the flag is Wales. The Union Jack can also be seen incorporated into the flags of other countries: Australia, New Zealand, Tuvalu, and Fiji.

Continent: Europe
Capital: London
Currency: pound sterling
Official language: English
Area: 93,628 sq. mi.
Highest point: Ben Nevis (4,406 ft.)

The United Kingdom is made up of four countries: England, Scotland, Wales, and Northern Ireland.

FRANCE

The day is July 14, 1789. The Bastille prison, in the center of Paris, is attacked by Parisian revolutionaries enraged by the policies of King Louis XVI. The revolutionaries wear badges called "cockades," which are blue and red, the same colors as the city of Paris. On the very next day, a decision is made to create a national flag, and the colors blue and red are chosen quite naturally. White is added to the mix, which symbolizes the French monarchy, yet it is placed in the middle, to signify that from now on, it will be the masses, and not the king, who have the power!

The tricolored French flag has served as a model for a number of countries who admire the French notions of liberty, equality, and fraternity.

Continent: Europe
Capital: Paris
Currency: euro
Official language: French
Area: 210,026 sq. mi.
Highest point: Mont Blanc (15,771 ft.)

The sansculottes, as the French revolutionaries were called, wore full-length trousers, unlike the aristocrats who donned stockings and knee breeches.

IRELAND

One must dive deep into the turbulent history of Ireland to understand the significance of the Irish flag. For centuries Ireland was mired in religious conflict. In the sixteenth century, Protestant England conquered Catholic Ireland: 97 percent of Ireland's lands were confiscated and appropriated by the Protestant colonists. The Irish people's civil and religious rights were stripped, and they could no longer practice their Catholic religion.

So what does this have to do with their flag?

Everything, as a matter of fact! Green is the color of the Catholic movement; orange is the color of the symbolic leader of the Protestants, William of Orange; and white, which links the two colors, symbolizes the hope for peace between the two religions. The Irish flag is a message of hope.

Continent: Europe
Capital: Dublin
Currency: euro
Official languages: English, Gaelic
Area: 27,133 sq. mi.
Highest point: Carrantuohill (3,414 ft.)

Every year on March 17, no matter where they are in the world, the Irish celebrate Saint Patrick, their patron saint.

LUXEMBOURG

Do you think France or the Netherlands inspired the flag of Luxembourg? If you pay close attention, you will notice that the three flags look a lot alike.

On the one hand, it has been said that the Luxembourgian flag copied the Dutch one. The explanation given is that, because both countries were governed by the same dynasty, the house of Orange-Nassau (1815–1890), Luxembourg was paying tribute to its former sovereign.

On the other hand, some people say that the drums of the French Revolution resonated as far as Luxembourg. The Grand Duchy, as the flag is called, paid homage to its neighbor's notions of freedom by adopting a tricolored flag.

So, which version do you believe?

Continent: Europe
Capital: Luxembourg
Currency: euro
Official languages: Luxembourgian, German, French
Area: 999 sq. mi.
Highest point: Buurgplaatz (1,834 ft.)

The Grand Ducal Palace is the residence of the Grand Duke, the leader of Luxembourg.

HUNGARY
Capital: Budapest

The Hungarian flag carries the trace of blood spilled by the Hungarian people. In homage to the French Revolution, the revolutionaries during the 1848 "Springtime of the Peoples" chose the colors red and white for their flag, but instead of using blue, they replaced it with green, a color on the Hungarian coat of arms. The folklore of the Romantic period assigned virtues to each color: red for power, white for faith, and green for hope.

AUSTRIA
Capital: Vienna

Legend has it that during the battle against the Moors, the Austrian Duke of Babenberg's white battledress became drenched in blood, except for the middle section, which was protected by his belt. Moved by the discovery, the duke decided to design his military banner in red and white. The striped banner was later adopted by the country for its national flag.

ROMANIA
Capital: Bucharest

In Romania, homeland of the famous Dracula, the national flag's colored stripes stand for the country's three historical provinces: Transylvania, Walachia, and Moldavia (though today only Moldavia's western half is still in Romania). The bold stripes are now unadorned, but the flag used to include the royal coat of arms, and later symbols of the Communist Party.

MOLDOVA
Capital: Chisinau

In Moldova, a country of steppes stretching out to the horizon, legend has it that Prince Dragos was hunting for aurochs (an ancestor of the cow) in the Carpathian Mountains. During the hunt, the prince's hound, Molda, drowned in a river, which Dragos named Moldova in his hound's honor. That name would soon extend to the country itself. The aurochs featured on the flag today is a reference to this legend.

NETHERLANDS

In the sixteenth century, the Republic of the United Provinces of the Netherlands was prosperous; the country's textile industry was booming and merchants in search of primary resources became interested in the Indies and the various treasures it had to offer, such as silk, spices, and tea. Ships soon embarked for South Africa, Indonesia, China, and as far away as Japan.

To establish his country's identity throughout the world, in 1584 Prince William of Orange decided to create a banner. He even gave it a name, the Prinsenvlag, or "the Prince's Flag." Nowadays, on national holidays, a thin orange banner is flown together with the tricolored flag in homage to the Orange family.

Continent: Europe
Capital: Amsterdam (official),
The Hague (seat of government)
Currency: euro
Official language: Dutch
Area: 16,040 sq. mi.
Highest point: Vaalserberg (1,053 ft.)

The Netherlands is the biggest exporter of plant bulbs in the world, especially tulips.

SPAIN

Red and yellow—the two oldest kingdoms of Spain (Castile in red and Aragon in yellow)—united to form the Spanish nation. Try to picture the marriage of Isabella of Castile and Ferdinand of Aragon in 1469: Isabella's subjects were dressed in gold and red; those of Ferdinand of Aragon wore yellow. And there you have the colors of the national flag!

Other royal kingdoms' coats of arms were later added to the flag: The castle represents Castile; the golden chains, Navarra; the grenadine (the fruit), the kingdom of Grenada; the four red stripes against a yellow background represent the crown of Aragon; the lion, the kingdom of Leon; and the three fleur-de-lis in the center symbolize the House of Bourbon-Anjou, which reigns in Spain to this day.

Continent: Europe
Capital: Madrid
Currency: euro
Official language: Spanish
Area: 194,845 sq. mi.
Highest point: Mulhacén (11,421 ft.)

The corrida (bullfight) is part of Spain's cultural heritage. The toreador confronts a bull wielding only a red cape and swords.

PORTUGAL

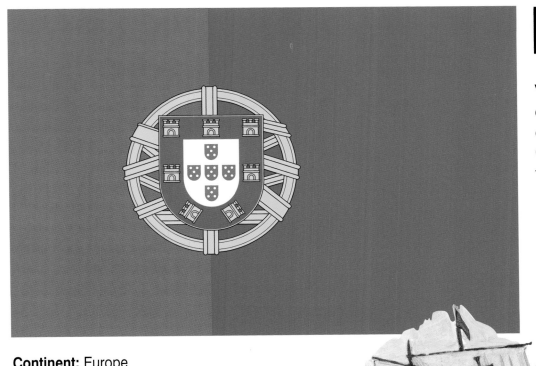

Vasco de Gama, the famous Portuguese explorer and naval commander who discovered a route to India by way of the Cape of Good Hope in Africa, may be familiar to you. But do you know the no-less-celebrated Dom Henrique, commonly known as Henry the Navigator?

His motto, "Go Beyond the Horizon," came about when he discovered the archipelagos of Madeira and Azores. Can you locate the armillary sphere on Portugal's flag? This navigational and astronomic tool evokes the great Portuguese explorers who crisscrossed the world in pursuit of uncharted territory. Situated on the Iberian Peninsula (the westernmost point on the European continent), Portugal and its sailors were at the forefront of global exploration.

Continent: Europe
Capital: Lisbon
Currency: euro
Official language: Portuguese
Area: 35,556 sq. mi.
Highest point: Serra da Estrela (6,541 ft.)

During the time of caravels (ships of the fifteenth and sixteenth centuries) the armillary sphere was an indispensable tool for navigation.

SAN MARINO

San Marino is among the smallest nations in Europe. You have to have an eagle eye to locate it on a map! Here's a clue: Find the northeast coast of the Italian boot and you will see a small area of land in the shape of a rough triangle hanging off the Apennine Mountains.

The combination of blue and white on the country's flag represents the snow of Mounte Titano (the highest mountain in San Marino) melting beneath the country's cloudless sky.

The center of the flag features the state's weaponry. Contrary to what you might expect, the crown doesn't symbolize monarchy, but rather the sovereignty of the people. In fact, San Marino is the oldest republic in the world, and the word *Libertas* symbolizes the will of the people in safeguarding their independence.

Continent: Europe
Capital: San Marino
Currency: euro
Official language: Italian
Area: 38 sq. mi.
Highest point: Mounte Titano (2,477 ft.)

One could easily pass through the tiny country of San Marino without even knowing it!

MALTA

The country of Malta is an archipelago situated in the middle of the Mediterranean Sea between Europe, the Middle East, and North Africa. Its strategic position has made it an important naval base in a number of conflicts.

White and red are the colors of the Order of Malta, a Catholic humanitarian organization that Charles I of Spain founded on the island in 1530.

During the Second World War, Malta fought alongside the Allies (France, the United Kingdom, and the United States). To pay tribute to the Maltese, King George VI of England awarded the country the George Cross, a replica of which appears in the top-left corner of the flag. It says, "For Gallantry."

Continent: Europe
Capital: Valletta
Currency: euro
Official languages: Maltese, English
Area: 122 sq. mi.
Highest point: Ta'Dmejrek (830 ft.)

The Sovereign Military Order of Malta is one of the oldest orders of the Catholic faith, providing service to the poor and sick.

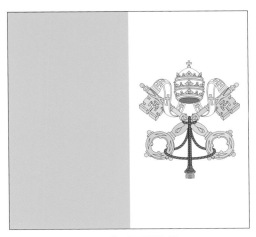

VATICAN CITY

Capital: Vatican City

In the contest for designation as the smallest country in Europe, **Vatican City** wins the gold prize. It measures a mere 0.2 square miles!

Monaco, located on the Mediterranean Sea, is a close second at 0.76 square miles.

Next up is **San Marino**, the oldest republic in the world, at 24 square miles.

Liechtenstein takes fourth place at 62 square miles.

Malta is next in line at 122 square miles.

Andorra is the biggest of the world's smallest nations, measuring 179 square miles.

MONACO Capital: Monaco

LIECHTENSTEIN

Capital: Vaduz

ANDORRA

Capital: Andorra la Vella

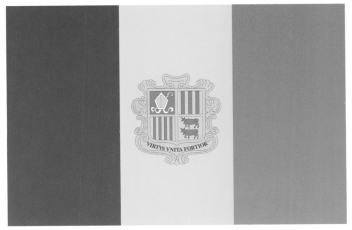

ITALY

The whole world knows Italy for its great artists, such as Michelangelo, Leonardo da Vinci, and Botticelli. And, of course, for its delicious pizza and spaghetti Bolognese. But the land of the "boot" (a nickname given to Italy because of its geographic shape), which has undergone many political and military struggles in its history, has an internationally known hero in Giuseppe Garibaldi, who fought for Italian independence. But while he's often called the "Hero of the Two Words," because he also engaged in revolutionary struggles in South America, Garibaldi wasn't behind the creation of Italy's flag. Like many flags around the world, the Italian flag was inspired by the French flag, which symbolizes the revolutionary values of liberty, equality, and fraternity. The Italian flag simply substitutes green for the blue of the French flag—some even claim that it was Napoleon Bonaparte who made that decision.

Continent: Europe
Capital: Rome
Currency: euro
Official language: Italian
Area: 116,346 sq. mi.
Highest point: Monte Bianco di Courmayeur (15,633 ft.)

Garibaldi, the "Hero of the Two Worlds."

SWITZERLAND

Switzerland has a very unusual flag, with its unique square shape and white cross at its center. Where does the cross come from?

Here's the history: In 1339 soldiers from Schweiz, a canton (a state in a federation) whose name means "Swiss" in German, left their country to defend Schweiz's freedom. A white cross was sewn on their uniforms to remind them of their native flag. Over time, the Swiss adopted this cross as a sign of peace and unity, since in this Alpine state, peace and neutrality in time of conflicts brought them prosperity.

Try not to confuse the Swiss flag with that of the Red Cross, whose colors are inversed (a red cross on a white background). The International Red Cross, founded by Henry Dunant in 1864, is widely regarded as the most important humanitarian organization in the world.

Continent: Europe
Capital: Bern
Currency: Swiss franc
Official languages: German, French, Italian, Romansh
Area: 15,940
Highest point: Dufourspitze (15,203 ft.)

The flag of the Red Cross, founded by the Swiss Henry Dunant, is the inverse of the Swiss flag.

GREECE

A typical Greek landscape features gleaming white buildings perched over the deep blue of the sea . . . these colors, inextricably linked to the country, are incorporated into Greece's flag in the form of nine blue and white stripes.

Do you think that this number was chosen at random? Hardly! It stands for the nine Greek syllables in the expression *Eleftheria i Thanatos* (meaning "Liberty or Death"), a rallying cry of independence against Turkish tyranny. After all, don't forget that the Turks ruled Greece until 1821.

And due to the country's Orthodox religion, a cross was also imbedded into the flag.

Continent: Europe
Capital: Athens
Currency: euro
Official language: Greek
Area: 50, 949 sq. mi.
Highest point: Mount Olympus (9,570 ft.)

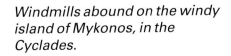

Windmills abound on the windy island of Mykonos, in the Cyclades.

45

CYPRUS

Is that the outline of the country on Cyprus's national flag? It is, and in fact Cyprus is the only country to feature its geographical shape on its flag.

So why does it appear in an ochre-yellow color? This island, situated in the Mediterranean near the Turkish coast, has been famous since Roman times for its stocks of copper, an orange-colored metal. What's more, the island was named after what the Romans called *aes cyprium*, which is the Latin name for copper.

Continent: Europe
Capital: Nicosia
Currency: euro
Official languages: Greek, Turkish
Area: 3,572 sq. mi.
Highest point: Mount Olympus (6,407 ft.)

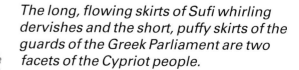

The long, flowing skirts of Sufi whirling dervishes and the short, puffy skirts of the guards of the Greek Parliament are two facets of the Cypriot people.

46

MONTENEGRO

Capital: Podgorica

ALBANIA Capital: Tirana

These are the flags of the former Yugoslavian countries.

In **Macedonia**, a great yellow sun shines over the people. Its representation on the flag symbolizes light, happiness, and freedom.

The flag of **Montenegro** features a crowned eagle, derived from the coat of arms of Nicolas I.

On **Albania's** flag, the eagle has two heads. According to legend, Albanians (the "eagle's sons") descended from this mythical bird.

The flag of **Bosnia-Herzegovina** is dominated by a golden triangle symbolizing hope and peace. This war-ravaged country adopted the colors and stars of the European Union.

MACEDONIA Capital: Skopje

BOSNIA-HERZEGOVINA

Capital: Sarajevo

48

THE AMERICAS

CANADA

Maple leaves turn red in autumn, which Canadians call "Indian summer." It's from this majestic tree that maple syrup is extracted. It's an appropriate symbol for this immense country, covered in large part by forests.

The snow-covered regions—the Inuit lands, the tundra, and Arctic savannah, as well as the lands around the Hudson Bay (the largest bay in the world)—are symbolized by the flag's white stripe. The red stripes pay tribute to the soldiers who perished in World War I. Did you know that the design of this flag required eighteen years of study and was chosen from more than fifteen hundred submissions?

Continent: North America
Capital: Ottawa
Currency: Canadian dollar
Official languages: English, French
Area: 3,855,103 sq. mi.
Highest point: Mount Logan (19,551 ft.)

To produce maple syrup, the tree's sap is extracted in the beginning of spring. When warmed, it becomes syrup.

UNITED STATES

There are fifty stars and thirteen stripes on this famous tricolored flag. The flag, nicknamed the "Stars and Stripes," is easily one of the most famous in the world.

The stars represent the number of states in the country. The last states to join were Alaska, bought from the Russians for a handful of dollars ($7,200,000), and Hawaii. They are the forty-ninth and fiftieth stars. There are thirteen stripes, corresponding to the thirteen original colonies in the Union. The white stripes signify honesty, and the red stripes, courage and fervor. The blue rectangle symbolizes loyalty, friendship, and justice. It's a beautiful message!

Continent: North America
Capital: Washington, D.C.
Currency: U.S. dollar
Official language: English
Area: 3,676,486 sq. mi.
Highest point: Mount McKinley
(20,335 ft., Alaska)

On July 20, 1969, the American astronaut Neil Armstrong walked on the surface of the moon and planted the American flag.

CUBA

Are you familiar with the "Caribbean Crocodile"? Don't be afraid—it's only the nickname given to the island of Cuba, due to its long shape. Now that would have made a fine image for the Cuban flag!

But it was the star of freedom that was ultimately chosen in 1902, to celebrate the country's independence, and so *la Estrella Solitaria* ("the solitary star") illuminates the path of the people toward freedom.

This flag was inspired by that of the United States, its big neighbor and even bigger foe. In Cuba's case, the blue stripes represent the country's three original provinces, whereas the white symbolizes the purity of revolutionary ideals and justice.

The famous revolutionary Fidel Castro ruled the island of Cuba from 1959 to 2008, when he was succeeded by his brother.

Region: West Indies
Capital: Havana
Currency: Cuban peso
Official language: Spanish
Area: 42,427 sq, mi.
Highest point: Pico Turquino (6,476 ft.)

Che Guevara, nicknamed "Che," fought alongside Fidel Castro, the former Cuban president, in the Cuban Revolution.

PANAMA
Capital: Panama City

In Panama, the Atlantic and Pacific Oceans, represented by the color blue on the flag, are linked by a canal that measures forty miles in length: the famous Panama Canal. The red and blue rectangles represent two of the country's major political parties, with white serving as a link between the two, as a sign of peace.

CHILE
Capital: Santiago

The color white was chosen for Chile's flag in order to symbolize the snow-covered peaks of the Andes Mountains, which extend over nearly 5,500 miles, from the southern tip of South America to its northern edge. In this flag, the sole star evokes the unity of the republic (unlike the United States, which features fifty stars on its flag, corresponding to its fifty different states).

PARAGUAY

Paraguay's is the only flag in the world with two different sides! The back doesn't look like the front. Couldn't the Paraguayans choose between the designs? They couldn't, because the two sides have very specific meanings.

On the obverse side, the "May Star" symbolizes independence from the Spanish in 1811. On the reverse side, a golden lion guards over a Phrygian cap, which symbolizes the defense of freedom. Does the Phrygian cap remind you of France? As a matter of fact, Paraguay adopted the three colors of the French flag, which is how it chose to express its admiration for the republican values embodied by the country of the "Declaration of the Rights of Man and of Citizens."

Continent: South America
Capital: Asunción
Currency: guaraní
Official languages: Spanish, Guaraní
Area: 157,048 sq. mi.
Highest point: Cerro San Rafael (2,789 ft.)

Paraguay, Brazil, and Argentina share the 275 waterfalls of Iguaçu, which extend over nearly two miles—nearly three times wider than Niagara Falls!

57

ANTIGUA AND BARBUDA

Ever since Antigua and Barbuda became an independent nation in 1967, its flag has represented nature: a beautiful rising sun with golden rays shining above blue waters (the color of the Caribbean) and white-sanded beaches. What a tempting invitation to a holiday!

The ebony-colored sky reflects the African origins of the slaves who once toiled in the country's sugar cane and tobacco fields. To mark the rupture with this somber past, two red triangles come together to form a *V*, evoking the word *victory*, which came through great sacrifice for this island state that had been part of the British Empire.

Region: West Indies
Capital: St. John's
Currency: Eastern Caribbean dollar
Official language: English
Area: 171 sq. mi.
Highest point: Boggy Peak (1,330 ft.)

The island's former landowners had brought over black slaves from West Africa to work in the plantations.

58

BAHAMAS

Welcome to paradise! Take shade under a coconut tree on a sandy beach, where the sea extends out as far as the eye can see. You're not dreaming—you're in the Bahamas. The yellow in the flag reminds us of the country's sandy beaches, and turquoise symbolizes the invariable color of the sea.

The black triangle evokes the African origins of the island's inhabitants. Liberated former slaves from other countries of North America, including Bermuda, arrived here in the seventeenth century. At that time, ships flying black pirate flags with skull and crossbones controlled the seas, searching for Spanish ships filled with gold and precious metals. Nowadays, we can sail peacefully between the islands of the Bahamas. But in New Providence still stands the lookout tower of the most famous pirate of his time: Blackbeard!

Region: Atlantic
Capital: Nassau
Currency: Bahamian dollar
Official language: English
Area: 5,382 sq. mi.
Highest point: Mount Alvernia (206 ft.)

Blackbeard became the leader of all the pirates in the region. He declared himself "magistrate of the privateers' republic."

DOMINICA

Take a look at the bird that has reigned supreme over the Dominican flag since 1988: The sisserou—a native parrot—is an endangered bird that exists nowhere else on Earth. When the country's political orientation shifted to socialism, the bird, which until then had faced right on the flag, turned to face the left: It did an about-face in accordance with the new power in place.

The cross symbolizes Christianity, or more specifically, the Trinity. Each of the three colors has a meaning: the white cross evokes the country's numerous waterfalls and rivers. The yellow cross, as bright as the sun, represents the native Caribbean Indians of the island, and the black cross, the African population who descended from slaves. The green background symbolizes the lush forests of this hot and humid region.

Region: West Indies
Capital: Roseau
Currency: Eastern Caribbean dollar
Official language: English
Area: 290 sq. mi.
Highest point: Morne Diablatins (4,747 ft.)

No, this plant isn't a palm tree—it's a fern tree! These tropical plants can reach over twenty feet in height!

SAINT LUCIA
Capital: Castries

Are you familiar with the Saint Lucian parrot that lives exclusively on the island of Saint Lucia? Probably not, as this bird has become quite rare. Here, sky and sea come together in the clear blue of the island's flag. The sharp, black triangle symbolizes the island's rocky peaks, some of which are volcanic. And the yellow in the middle represents the golden sand of its serene beaches.

BARBADOS
Capital: Bridgetown

On Barbados's flag, golden sand, symbolized by the color yellow, is surrounded by an intense blue, which evokes the ocean. Does the trident in the center mean that the water is brimming with fish? Most probably, since this spear is used to harpoon fish. It also symbolizes the sea: Neptune, the Roman god of the oceans, is always represented with a trident in his hand.

MEXICO

Centuries ago, in 1325 to be exact, the people living in the north of Mexico searched for the ideal location to build a new city. The Aztec god Huitzilopochtli had prophesized that they would receive a sign, indicating the spot where their celebrated city should be. Everything happened as predicted: An eagle carrying a snake in its beak descended from the sky and landed upon a prickly pear, and there the nomads built their city, naming it Tenochtitlan, which would later become Mexico City, the capital of Mexico.

This is the legend reproduced in the center of the Mexican flag.

Continent: North America
Capital: Mexico City
Currency: Mexican peso
Official language: Spanish
Area: 758,450 sq. mi.
Highest peak: Pico de Orizaba (18,701 ft.)

The Aztecs founded a great empire in the fifteenth century. Their great architectural talent is evident in their pyramids.

BOLIVIA

Have you heard of La Paz, the capital of Bolivia? At an altitude of over 12,000 feet, it's the highest city in the world! From the altiplano (high plain), at 12,500 feet, to the great plains of the northeast, Bolivia's subsoil is rich with minerals: Tin, silver, oil, and gas are the primary resources of this ancient Incan country. These treasures are extremely valuable and are proudly represented on the nation's flag by a yellow stripe. The country's flag also celebrates Bolivia's fertile soil, in which tobacco, sugar cane, bananas, and coca are grown; this is represented by the green stripe. The bright red stripe symbolizes the courage of the Bolivian people, as well as their sense of sacrifice and love for their country. Have you noticed the striking resemblance between the flags of Bolivia and Ghana? Fortunately for our memories, Ghana's flag has a star.

Continent: South America
Capital: La Paz
Currency: boliviano
Official languages: Spanish, Quechua, Aymara
Area: 424,164
Highest point: Nevado Sajama (21,463 ft.)

Situated at an altitude of 12,500 feet above sea level, Lake Titicaca is the highest navigable lake in the world.

PERU

"There goes the flag of liberty!" cried General José San Martin upon observing a school of pink flamingoes, great wading birds with white chests and wings hemmed with red. It has been said that the idea for Peru's national flag came about during the war against Spain in 1820. The coat of arms pays tribute to the country's flora and fauna: The tree on the right is a cinchona, which is used to treat malaria, an illness transmitted by insects that can lead to severe fever. At the left, the llama is a symbol of the Andes Cordillera, a massive mountain chain that crosses the country. Underneath, the horn of plenty evokes the natural riches of this ancient Incan empire.

Continent: South America
Capital: Lima
Currency: nuevo sol
Official languages: Spanish, Quechua, Aymara
Area: 496,218 sq. mi.
Highest point: Nevado Huascarán (22,205 ft.)

Flamingoes are large birds, measuring up to five feet tall. Their pink hue is derived from the crustaceans upon which they feed.

COSTA RICA

Two ships at sail express Costa Rica's ambition to conquer the world at sea. These two ships straddle the country, with the Caribbean Sea on one side and the Pacific Ocean on the other. The three mountains represent the three mountain ranges of Costa Rica. Did you know that there are still some active volcanoes in this country? It's best not to get too close to them!

It has been said that the country's red stripe symbolizes Costa Rica's admiration for revolutionary France. The country itself is represented by a white stripe, indicating its location between the Atlantic and Pacific Oceans, which are symbolized by blue.

Continent: North America
Capital: San José
Currency: Costa Rican colón
Official language: Spanish
Area: 19,730 sq. mi.
Highest point: Cerro Chirripó (12,530 ft.)

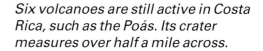

Six volcanoes are still active in Costa Rica, such as the Poás. Its crater measures over half a mile across.

66

HONDURAS Capital: Tegucigalpa

Do you know why all of these countries adopted two blue stripes and one white stripe on their flags?

Simply because in the nineteenth century, they were all members (along with Costa Rica) of a federation called the **United Provinces of Central America**. As a sign of unity, they incorporated the same colors in their flags. White represents Central America, and blue represents the two oceans, one on each coast—just like on the map!

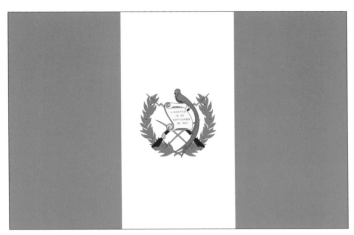

GUATEMALA
Capital: Guatemala City

EL SALVADOR
Capital: San Salvador

NICARAGUA Capital: Managua

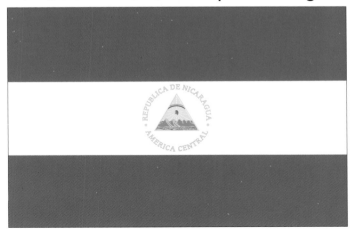

BELIZE

Sub umbra floreo ("Under the shade I flourish") is the motto that appears on Belize's flag. This should come as no surprise for a country whose land is half-covered in tropical forests. The mahogany tree that can be distinguished in the center of the coat of arms is the country's primary natural resource. Its red-colored wood is used to build furniture, violins, and guitars.

The ax, saw, paddle, and ship represent the country's woodworking and marine activities. And because the population of Belize is made up of black, white, and mixed-race people, the coat of arms depicts both a white man and a black man.

Continent: North America
Capital: Belmopan
Currency: Belize dollar
Official language: English
Area: 8,867 sq. mi.
Highest point: Victoria Peak (3,681 ft.)

Belize's forests contain mahogany trees. Many people seek the trees' dense, valuable wood.

ARGENTINA

The sun shines brightly on the flag of Argentina! It has a name: El Sol de Mayo ("the Sun of May"), which marks the first day of the battle for independence, in May 1810. But don't let it fool you. It snows quite a bit in this Andean nation, as symbolized by the flag's white stripe. Argentina runs alongside 3,100 miles of the Andes Cordillera, the longest mountain range in the world!

The clear, pure sky above the great regions of the Pampa, Tierra del Fuego, and Patagonia also leaves its mark on the national flag.

As you may have noticed, the Argentine flag greatly inspired that of its neighbor, Uruguay.

Continent: South America
Capital: Buenos Aires
Currency: Argentine peso
Official language: Spanish
Area: 1,073,520 sq. mi.
Highest point: Cerro Aconcagua (22,831 ft.)

Tango was born in Argentina at the end of the nineteenth century, in Buenos Aires. This dance involves two people, and can occur in cafés or even in the street.

URUGUAY

You may have noticed that the Uruguayan flag is very similar to the flag of its Argentine neighbor situated on the opposite bank of Rio de la Plata, one of the longest rivers in the world.

The nine blue and white stripes symbolize the nine original provinces that make up this country, which was once a Spanish colony. Contrary to Argentina, it never snows in this South American country. On the other hand, the "Sun of May," which is the country's national motto, shines above Uruguay for the same reasons as it does Argentina. A revolutionary symbol par excellence, it brilliantly evokes the country's independence from Spanish rule in May 1828.

Continent: South America
Capital: Montevideo
Currency: Uruguayan peso
Official language: Spanish
Area: 68,679 sq. mi.
Highest point: Cerro Catedral (1,685 ft.)

Gauchos, cowboys on horseback, are numerous in Uruguay as three-quarters of the country is covered in pastures.

71

ECUADOR

The Andean condor stretches its wings over the eternal snows of Chimborazo. At 20,702 feet, it is the highest volcano in the world.

Welcome to Ecuador! The flag's coat of arms invites us to discover the country's sumptuous landscapes, located between the mountains and the sea. The Pacific Ocean, the rivers, and the sky are represented by the flag's dark blue stripe. If you prefer to get to know the country by navigating a small boat down the Guayas River, you're more than welcome to! The country's natural resources and prosperity radiate out from the large yellow stripe. And the red memorializes the blood spilled by the country's patriots, who brought freedom to the nation. These three colors descend from the Gran Colombia, a confederation formed during the independence from Spain (1821–1830), encompassing Venezuela, Panama, and Colombia.

Continent: South America
Capital: Quito
Currency: U.S. dollar
Official language: Spanish
Area: 105,037 sq. mi.
Highest point: Chimborazo (20,702 ft.)

At the Quito market, peasants still wear traditional dress — and the hat is essential, even for women!

72

COLOMBIA
Capital: Bogotá

In the early nineteenth century, Ecuador, Colombia, Venezuela, and for a while Panama, formed the Gran Colombia, after each nation achieved its independence from Spain. As a sign of unity, the countries' flags adopted the same colors: the Atlantic Ocean (in blue), separated the Spanish oppressor (in red and yellow) from the rich Americas.

VENEZUELA
Capital: Caracas

Eight stars shine brightly on the flag of Venezuela. The first seven correspond to the seven provinces that signed the independence act in 1806. The eighth star, added in March 2006, pays tribute to the memory of a national hero, Simón Bolivar. Beginning in 1813, this man fought for the emancipation of Spanish colonies in Latin America.

GRENADA

The kindness and courtesy of the people of Grenada are illustrated in their flag in the form of two big triangles, grapefruit-yellow like the fruit that is grown there. Banana trees, sugar cane fields, cacao trees, spices . . . all the country's agriculture and fertile soil are symbolized by two green triangles.

In Grenada, nutmeg, which lends a very special flavor to local cuisine, is an institution. It is the symbol that appears on the flag in yellow and red. In fact, Grenada is the second-largest producer of nutmeg in the world.

Region: West Indies
Capital: St. George's
Currency: Eastern Caribbean dollar
Official language: English
Area: 133 sq. mi.
Highest point: Mount Saint Catherine (2,756 ft.)

In mid-August, parades abound throughout the country. Mardi Gras and Dimanche Gras are just two of the holidays celebrated there.

GUYANA

Nature takes center stage on the flag of Guyana. As three-quarters of the country is covered by spectacular forests, and sugar cane plantations run alongside paddy fields, green was chosen as the dominant color. The subsoil also offers its share of riches: bauxite, gold, and diamonds are represented by the yellow triangle, while the white edge evokes the numerous waterfalls and rivers that irrigate the country's agricultural fields.

But the country's natural riches would not have amounted to much without the tenacity and patience of its people. The red triangle outlined in black was chosen to pay homage to the island's inhabitants.

Continent: South America
Capital: Georgetown
Currency: Guyanese dollar
Official language: English
Area: 83,012 sq. mi.
Highest point: Mount Roraima (9,301 ft.)

This mountainous country is overflowing with waterfalls. Kaieteur Falls, on the Potaro River, measure 741 feet in height.

SURINAME

Much like its neighbor Guyana's flag, Suriname's pays tribute to the tremendous forests that cover 95 percent of this country's surface. The two green stripes reflect the rich vegetation of this South American country, including its grassy prairies brimming with cattle and sheep and its sugar cane fields.

Situated on the edge of the Atlantic Ocean, Suriname has welcomed people coming from distant horizons: Indians, Indonesians, Japanese, Creoles, Chinese, and Amerindians. All of them are joined together in the center of the flag in the form of a yellow star, which symbolizes their hope for unity and peace. The white stripes also evoke peace, freedom, and justice. A beautiful combination!

Continent: South America
Capital: Paramaribo
Currency: Suriname dollar
Official language: Dutch
Area: 63,251 sq. mi.
Highest point: Juliana Top (4,035 ft.)

In Suriname's swamps, mangrove trees, which have elevated roots, form strange forests.

SAINT VINCENT
AND THE GRENADINES
Capital: Kingstown

The color of the sun shines brightly in the center of this flag. Blue evokes the island's crystal-clear waters and green stands for its lush vegetation. In the center, the diamond shapes represent the three islands of this country, as well as the serrated leaves of the breadfruit tree.

JAMAICA
Capital: Kingston

The colors of Jamaica are yellow (for the sun and country's riches) and green (for its vegetation); yet black also makes an appearance on the country's flag, to evoke its oppression and poverty. The reggae singer Bob Marley is undoubtedly the country's most famous native son, spreading Jamaica's colors to the world, namely Ethiopia.

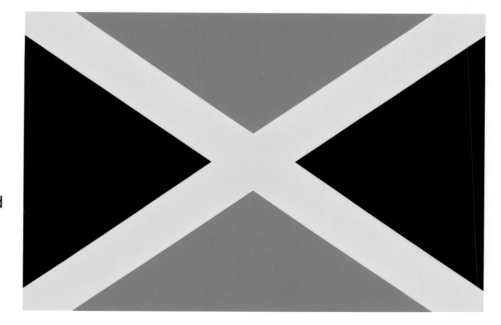

TRINIDAD
AND TOBAGO
Capital: Port of Spain

The flag of Trinidad and Tobago, a significant producer of oil, asphalt, and natural gas, celebrates its rich natural resources by way of a large, diagonal black stripe. Black also represents the strong links that unite the inhabitants of these two islands. Additionally, white symbolizes the sea and red represents the sun.

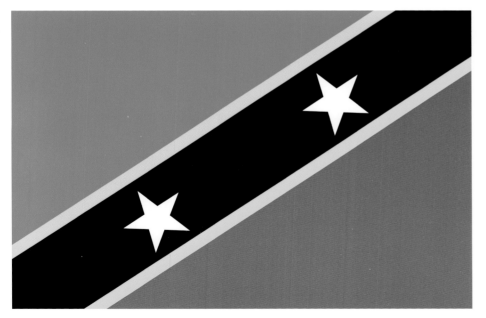

SAINT KITTS
AND NEVIS
Capital: Basseterre

In Saint Kitts and Nevis's flag, the fertility of the land is represented by the color green: Here, the sugar cane crop reigns supreme. Red symbolizes the struggle against slavery and colonialism. The black diagonal line evokes the African heritage of the population. And the stars stand for the two islands of this archipelago.

DOMINICAN REPUBLIC

Once upon a time, after Christopher Columbus discovered the Caribbean in 1492, two nations—the Dominican Republic and Haiti—peacefully shared an island named Hispaniola.

Unfortunately, that harmony didn't last, and the two nations ended up fighting over the land. Haiti eventually became the ruler of the Dominican Republic. But even after the latter achieved independence, its flag was still modeled after Haiti's. The Dominicans simply added a large white cross to convey their religious devotion. Furthermore, the flag's coat of arms features an open Bible and the motto "God, Fatherland, Liberty"— three words very dear to the people.

Region: West Indies
Capital: Santo Domingo
Currency: Dominican peso
Official language: Spanish
Area: 18,792 sq. mi.
Highest point: Pico Duarte (10,417 ft.)

Each year humpback whales migrate to the warm waters of the Caribbean to spawn.

HAITI

"Unity Makes Strength" is the motto that appears on the Haitian flag, representing the Haitian population's descendance from African slaves and people of both European and African ancestries. The two colors on the national flag stand for these two communities.

The cohesion of the communities was essential, even at the high cost of using force. The country's coat of arms depicts cannons and cannonballs, completing the portrait of a nation with a chaotic past.

Region: West Indies
Capital: Port-au-Prince
Currency: gourde
Official languages: Haitian Creole, French
Area: 10,695 sq. mi.
Highest point: Mount Selle (8,773 ft.)

Once roasted, Haitian coffee beans give off a very unique aroma. Their export has become an indispensable source of revenue for the country.

BRAZIL

Can you speak Portuguese? If not, it doesn't matter; the national motto depicted on the Brazilian flag, *Ordem e Progresso*, is easy to understand: "Order and Progress."

As Brazil is the largest country in South America, its tropical forest is also the largest in the world. It grows on the banks of the Amazon River—the largest river in the world!—covering more than a third of the country, which was once colonized by the Portuguese. The country's flag reflects this rich vegetation: the color green covers almost its entire surface.

The flag's most unusual property is undoubtedly the starry sky. It has been said that this was the exact configuration of the stars in 1889, the year Brazil proclaimed itself a republic. In addition, the twenty-seven stars represent the twenty-six states of the Brazilian federation, plus one for its capital, Brasília.

Continent: South America
Capital: Brasília
Currency: Brazilian real
Official language: Portuguese
Area: 3,287,612 sq. mi.
Highest point: Pico da Neblina (9,888 ft.)

The Amazonian Indians are threatened by extinction due to the excessive deforestation of their habitat.

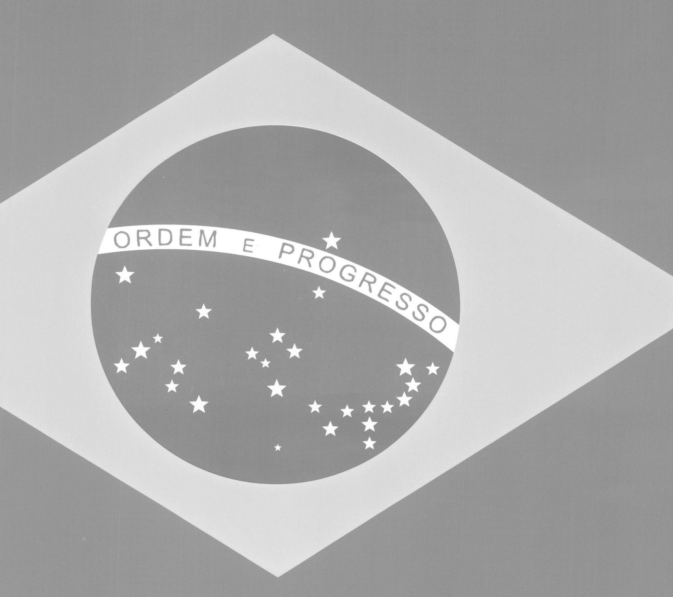

OCEANIA

AUSTRALIA

With an area of 2,969,978 square miles, Australia is the largest island in the world! You may be wondering why the British flag—the Union Jack—appears on Australia's flag. It is because Captain Cook, an Englishman, took possession of the island in 1770.

Six stars are represented on the flag: The first five make up the Southern Cross, the most commonly known constellation in the Southern Hemisphere. The sixth star, which is larger than the others and slightly off-center, represents Australia itself, an island situated between the Pacific and Indian Oceans.

But these six stars also denote the six states that make up Australia: Queensland and its Great Barrier Reef, South Australia, New South Wales, Western Australia, Tasmania, and Victoria.

Region: Oceania
Capital: Canberra
Currency: Australian dollar
Official language: English
Area: 2,969,978 sq. mi.
Highest point: Mount Kosciuszko (7,310 ft.)

In 1770 Captain James Cook discovered the southern coast of Australia from his ship, the Endeavor.

NEW ZEALAND

Do you notice a resemblance here? It seems as if we are in England again: same colors, same Union Jack in the upper-left corner. Perhaps this makes sense for a former British colony. With its fjords, lakes, glaciers, geysers, and volcanoes, this archipelago and its diverse landscape is today part of the Commonwealth (the confederation of nations that were formerly part of the British Empire).

On this flag, the Southern Cross (the most commonly known constellation in the Southern Hemisphere) seems to have lost a star! There are only four. But that's to distinguish New Zealand's flag from the flag belonging to neighboring Australia, which is practically identical.

Region: Oceania
Capital: Wellington
Currency: New Zealand dollar
Official languages: English, Maori
Area: 104,515 sq. mi.
Highest point: Mount Cook (12,316 ft.)

The Maori, who came from Polynesia more than twelve hundred years ago, are the oldest inhabitants of New Zealand.

TUVALU
Capital: Funafuti

The British flag was hoisted over the vast sky-blue waters of Fiji and Tuvalu to signal their membership in the Commonwealth. On Tuvalu's flag, the Union Jack—the British flag—is placed next to nine yellow stars, which represent the nine islands of this archipelago nation, one of the smallest and most isolated in the world, situated in the center of the Pacific Ocean.

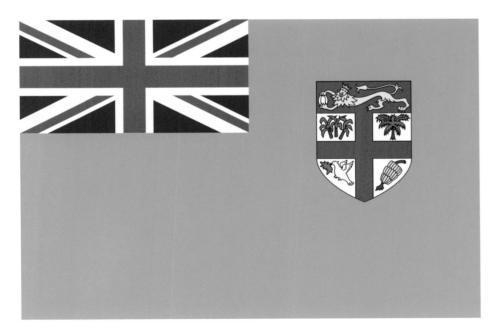

FIJI
Capital: Suva

On Fiji's flag, the British flag is placed next to national emblems: a coconut palm, bananas, and sugar cane—the principal agricultural products of this volcanic archipelago. A white dove, a symbol of peace, appears along with the British lion, which reflects the strong relationship between the two countries.

MARSHALL ISLANDS

The ultramarine blue background of this flag stands for the ocean, which surrounds this island nation containing thirty-two low-lying atolls. The most famous of them is the Bikini atoll, which gave its name to the two-piece swimsuit in the 1950s!

The flag's star shines as brightly as the sun and is a symbol of the country. Its twenty-eight rays represent the state's twenty-four electoral districts, while Christianity, the country's predominant religion, is illustrated by the four largest rays, which form a cross.

Region: Oceania
Capital: Majuro
Currency: U.S. dollar
Official languages: English, Marshallese
Area: 70 sq. mi.
Highest point: 33 ft.

Corals aren't plants— they're animals that form colonies in warm seas.

NAURU

Thanks to its national flag, Nauru's geographical location is easy to find: near the equator! The yellow stripe that crosses through the center symbolizes this imaginary line that divides the Earth into two hemispheres. The white, twelve-pointed star represents the twelve indigenous tribes on the island. The island's population is concentrated along the coasts, forming an almost-continuous urban ribbon about the island.

John Fearn, who discovered the Polynesian atoll in 1798, called it Pleasant Island, and for a long time the island was a terrestrial paradise, brimming with lush vegetation. Unfortunately, after years of mining its natural resources, humans have severely damaged the island's idyllic landscapes, and all but exhausted its reserves.

Region: Oceania
Capital: Yaren
Currency: Australian dollar
Official languages: Nauruan, English
Area: 8.2 sq. mi.
Highest point: 213 ft.

Nauru is an atoll, an island of coral that surrounds a lagoon (a body of shallow water).

KIRIBATI

Kiribati's flag looks like a postcard: A golden sun in the scarlet red sky rises up over the blue and white waves of the Pacific Ocean. In the glowing red horizon flies a frigate bird, that mythical great bird of Oceania symbolizing authority and liberty.

   Did you know that until 1995, this country, dispersed over more than 1,351,000 square miles, was located directly over the International Date Line? That meant that when it was Monday on one island, it was Tuesday on a neighboring island! The date line was shifted to ensure that all of Kiribati had its Monday at the same time.

Region: Oceania
Capital: Tarawa
Currency: Australian dollar
Official language: English
Area: 313 sq. mi. (land)
Highest point: Banaba Island (285 ft.)

The clown fish calls Kiribati's waters home. This unusual fish lives in close association with poisonous anemones; once an anemone has been adopted, the clownfish defends it vigorously, in return gaining a safe home within its stinging tentacles.

PAPUA NEW GUINEA

Papua New Guinea occupies the eastern half of the island of New Guinea. Can you guess who designed this archipelago's flag? A fifteen-year-old girl who won a nationwide competition for the flag's design! Her inspiration came from the island's many amazing features.

The red triangle evokes the lush vegetation and humid climate of the country. The black triangle represents the island's volcanic soil. What about the beautiful yellow bird, called the Raggi's bird-of-paradise? It's the symbol of the island, as the bird is found nowhere else but here. It is facing the Southern Cross, the best-known constellation in the Southern Hemisphere, containing five stars. Papua New Guinea is known for having the greatest linguistic diversity in the world. It is home to more than 750 dialects!

Region: Oceania
Capital: Port Moresby
Currency: kina
Official language: English
Area: 178,704 sq. mi.
Highest point: Mount Wilhelm (14,793 ft.)

Some tribal Papuans build houses in trees at heights of up to 160 feet in order to protect themselves from danger.

PALAU Capital: Melekeok

Nature is ever present on these flags!

The yellow circle of **Palau's** flag represents the full moon, which regulates the lives of Palauans during harvest and celebrations.

The Y-shaped mountainous and volcanic archipelago of **Vanuatu** is reflected on its flag.

The stars of **Micronesia's** flag represent the nation's four island groups dispersed in the blue of the Pacific Ocean.

On the **Solomon Islands'** flag, the sun, vegetation, and ocean are represented by yellow, green, and blue!

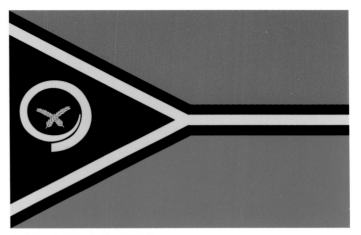

VANUATU Capital: Port Vila

MICRONESIA Capital: Palikir

SOLOMON ISLANDS
Capital: Honiara

SAMOA

This country, situated in the heart of the South Pacific, chose to depict the stars of the Southern Cross in the upper-left corner of its flag. Samoa's location in the Southern Hemisphere makes it one of the best places to observe the five stars of this famous constellation.

The color red dominates the flag; this is perhaps due to the volcanic nature of the archipelago, which provides a favorable climate for growing pineapples and bananas, both valuable crops for the country.

An independent monarchy since 1962, this country also belongs to the Commonwealth, the confederation of the former British colonies.

Region: Oceania
Capital: Apia
Currency: tala
Official languages: Samoan, English
Area: 1,093 sq. mi.
Highest point: Mauga Silisili (6,095 ft.)

The volcanic archipelago of Samoa is an important producer of pineapples.

TONGA

Toupu IV, the king of Tonga, wanted to illustrate the religious devotion of his country's inhabitants on the national flag. To do so, he chose a cross to represent this archipelago of 170 islands. Red evokes the blood of Christ and white is for purity. But does this symbol give you a sense of déjà vu? It's the Red Cross, of course! When Henry Dunant created the international organization in 1863, he chose as his logo a red cross, identical to the one that Tonga had adopted for its flag shortly beforehand.

To avoid confusion, in 1875 the white rectangle with the red cross was moved to the upper left-hand corner of Tonga's flag: By doing so, it was no longer the central motif of the flag, just a detail.

Region: Oceania
Capital: Nuku'alofa
Currency: pa'anga
Official languages: Tongan, English
Area: 290 sq. mi.
Highest point: Mount Kao (3,389 ft.)

Agriculture is Tonga's primary source of revenue; vanilla, passion fruit, and cassava are grown locally.

AFRICA

SWAZILAND

One thing is for sure: The warriors of the Emasotsha Regiment keep watch over Swaziland! The country's emblem is composed of a bold portrayal of a traditional cowhide shield, reinforced by Zulu warrior spears and a ceremonial stick decorated with feathers and tassels. It's a very unusual flag.

But why display symbols of battle and violence on a national flag? It turns out that the Swazi people took up arms quite often during the course of their history; the shield and spears symbolize protection from the country's enemies. But the colors black and white stand for the good relationship between the country's black and white communities.

This miniscule, mountainous country is so proud of its battle victories that it decorated its flag with traditional instruments of power.

Continent: Africa
Capital: Mbabane
Currency: lilangeni
Official languages: Swati, English
Area: 6,704 sq. mi.
Highest point: Mount Emlembe (6,109 ft.)

The indlamu, *a traditional Zulu war dance, follows a vigorous rhythm.*

100

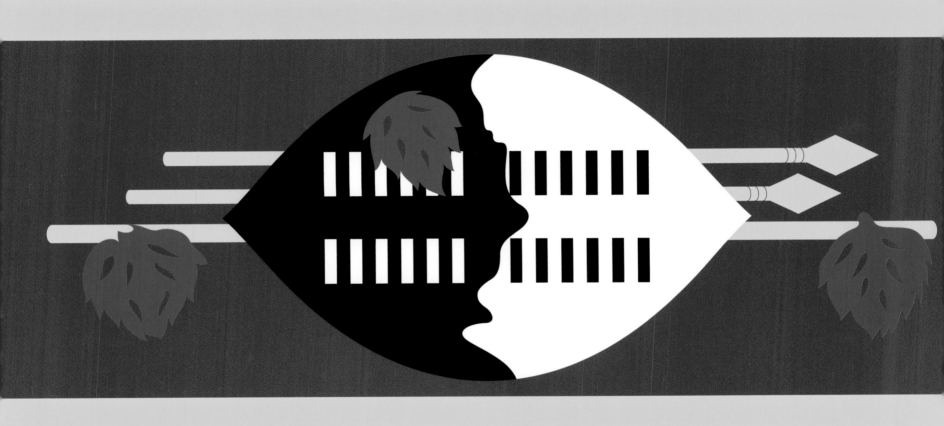

MOROCCO

Red is an appropriate color for the Moroccan flag! For centuries, the sultans of Morocco have used red to proclaim their direct descent from the prophet Mohammed, founder of Islam. The green pentagram, a star with five points that is also known as the Seal of Solomon, was added long ago to distinguish the Moroccan flag from the flags of other Muslim countries that at one time were red. Each point of the star represents one of the five pillars of Islam: profession of faith, prayer, alms giving, fasting, and pilgrimage to Mecca.

Continent: Africa
Capital: Rabat
Currency: Moroccan dirham
Official language: Arabic
Area: 177,117 sq. mi.
Highest point: Djebel Toubkal (13,665 ft.)

Muslims pray five times a day facing Mecca. Daily prayer is one of the five pillars of Islam.

102

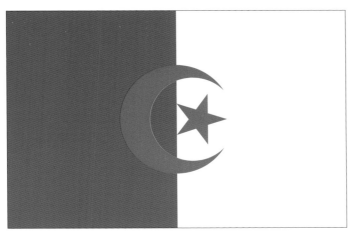

ALGERIA Capital: Algiers

Look closely at the following four flags and concentrate on their similarities. In your opinion, what do they have in common?

The **crescent moon**, of course! These four countries are Islamic, and the moon has a very important place in Islam. The Islamic calendar has 354 days and is based on the motion of the moon. The position of the moon in the sky determines the date of the pilgrimage to Mecca and of Ramadan, the Islamic time of fasting.

TUNISIA Capital: Tunis

MAURITANIA
Capital: Nouakchott

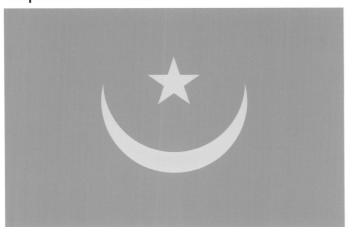

COMOROS Capital: Moroni

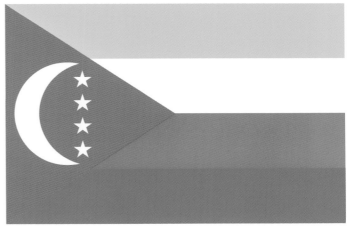

EGYPT

You may have heard of Tutankhamen, Nefertiti, Cleopatra, or even the Karnak Temple or the Valley of the Kings. But what about the golden eagle that reigns majestically over the Egyptian flag? This is the crest that the Sultan Saladin chose to symbolize his power. In the twelfth century, Saladin founded the Ayyubid dynasty, which would reign over Egypt and Syria for nearly a century. In 1984, Egypt adopted this triumphal crest to demonstrate the country's supremacy.

The Egyptian flag also introduces us to the family of flags incorporating the Pan-Arab colors of red, black, and white. Pan-Arab countries share a common political language and hail from the Arab civilization.

In early 2011, a local uprising succeeded in overturning President Mubarak's regime after a thirty-year reign. Today, Egypt is experiencing a delicate transition period toward a new political system.

The Pyramid of Khafre still holds a number of unsolved mysteries.

Continent: Africa
Capital: Cairo
Currency: Egyptian pound
Official language: Arabic
Area: 385,229 sq. mi.
Highest point: Mount Saint Catherine (8,668 ft.)

104

SUDAN and SOUTH SUDAN

Until July 9, 2011, Sudan and South Sudan were one country. That day marked the official separation of the southern and northern parts of the country, which had been fighting a bloody civil war for many years. Sudan kept the original flag, whose Pan-Arab colors (red, white, black, and green) proclaim its adherence to its Arab-Muslim roots. South Sudan chose the flag used by the People's Liberation Army in their fight for independence. The bands of colors symbolize the South Sudanese people (black), peace (white), the blood spilled for liberty (red), and the homeland (green). The blue of the triangle evokes the Nile River, while the gold star symbolizes unity.

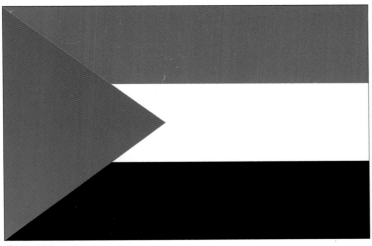

SUDAN
Continent: Africa
Capital: Khartoum
Currency: Sudanese pound
Official language: Arabic
Area: 728,215 sq. mi.
Highest point: Jebel Marra (9,980 ft.)

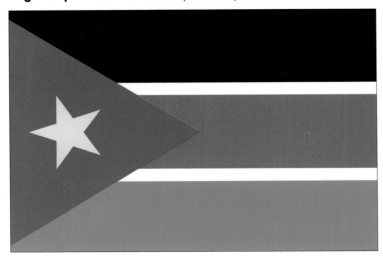

SOUTH SUDAN
Continent: Africa
Capital: Juba
Currency: South Sudanese pound
Official language: Arabic
Area: 239,285 sq. mi.
Highest point: Mont Kinyeti (10,456 ft.)

ETHIOPIA

Did you know that Ethiopia is known as the cradle of humanity? This is due to the early human remains found in the Omo Valley, in the heart of the country, between high plateaus, swamps, and savannahs. Ethiopia is one of the oldest nations in the world.

In this country known for its droughts, the color green represents hope, particularly the hope for more fertile ground. Yellow, the color of the sun, brings joy. As for red, it denotes the strength and courage of the people in defending freedom.

Ethiopia, invaded and occupied by Italy for only six years, is the only African country to have resisted colonization in the nineteenth century. The main three colors of its flag have become emblematic and have brought hope to a number of African countries.

Continent: Africa
Capital: Addis Ababa
Currency: birr
Official language: Amharic
Area: 435,186 sq. mi.
Highest point: Ras Dashen (15,157 ft.)

The Rasta cultural movement (or Rastafari) adopted the colors of the Ethiopian flag.

GHANA

This country, discovered by the Portuguese in the fifteenth century, is an El Dorado: Gold is everywhere! Later on, the British called the country the Gold Coast.

Ghana adopted the colors red, yellow, and green to celebrate its independence in 1957. The black star in the center is a symbol of victory and freedom. But did you know that Ghana wasn't the first to adopt these colors? Ethiopia chose them first. And as Ethiopia was the first African country to escape colonization, these three stripes (called the Pan-African colors) were eventually adopted by other countries in Africa, such as Guinea, Mali, Senegal, and Guinea-Bissau.

Continent: Africa
Capital: Accra
Currency: cedi
Official language: English
Area: 92,098 sq. mi.
Highest point: Mount Afadjato (2,903 ft.)

A village chief proudly wears a golden crown. Ghana was called the Gold Coast due to its abundance of this metal.

108

GUINEA Capital: Conakry

MALI Capital: Bamako

GUINEA-BISSAU Capital: Bissau

SENEGAL Capital: Dakar

TOGO
Capital: Lomé

On the flag of Togo, a country of golden beaches studded with coconut palms, the yellow stripes symbolize the richness of its subsoil: This West African country is the world's fifth-largest producer of phosphate, which is used as a fertilizer for crops. The hope and wisdom of the Togolese is reflected in the flag's star, as white is the color of purity.

SÃO TOMÉ
AND PRÍNCIPE
Capital: São Tomé

The archipelago of São Tomé and Príncipe consists of two volcanic islands off the coast of Gabon. These islands are symbolized by two black stars on the flag. The country's lush vegetation is represented by the color green.

BENIN Capital: Porto-Novo

BURKINA FASO Capital: Ouagadougou

REPUBLIC OF THE CONGO
Capital: Brazzaville

CAMEROON Capital: Yaoundé

EQUATORIAL GUINEA

Equatorial Guinea shows off its natural richness on its flag, namely its dense, immense forests. When its forests contain exotic kapok (or silk cotton) trees, why not be proud?

The kapok tree is gigantic. Its cylindrical trunk can grow to heights of up to 160 feet! Nicknamed the "tree of God," it seems to touch the sky.

According to legend, King Bonkoro I signed the first treaty of allegiance with Spain, its former colonizer, underneath this tree.

The country's coat of arms also features six yellow stars representing the continental region and the five offshore islands. Beneath the coat of arms is the national motto in Spanish: *Unidad, Paz, Justicia* ("Unity, Peace, Justice").

Continent: Africa
Capital: Malabo
Currency: Central African CFA franc
Official languages: Spanish, French
Area: 10,831 sq. mi.
Highest point: Pico Basile (9,869 ft.)

Kapok is a kind of fiber found in the seedpods of the kapok tree.

FLAGS OF MANY COUNTRIES—

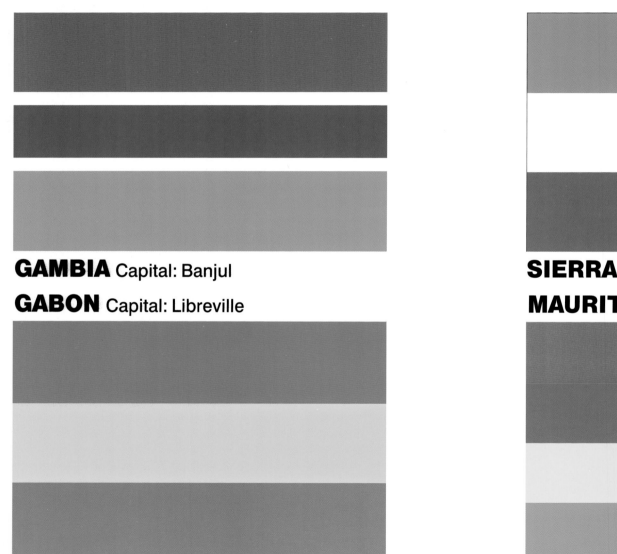

GAMBIA Capital: Banjul

GABON Capital: Libreville

SIERRA LEONE Capital: Freetown

MAURITIUS Capital: Port Louis

A MULTITUDE OF STRIPES AND COLORS

NIGERIA Capital: Abuja

CHAD Capital: N'Djamena

CÔTE D'IVOIRE Capital: Abidjan

ZAMBIA Capital: Lusaka

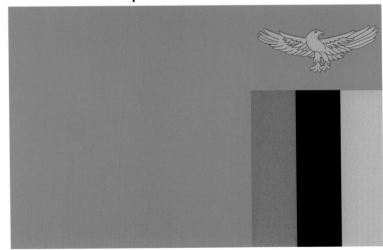

TANZANIA

In your opinion, what is the significance of the diagonal line that divides the Tanzanian flag into two halves? Does it refer to the geography of the country? No, the triangles do. On one side, the green triangle represents the abundant vegetation of the plains and forests bordering the famous Rift Valley. On the other side, the blue triangle stands for the Indian Ocean, which borders the country and its legendary island of Zanzibar.

The black stripe is actually a tribute to the native black people of Tanzania and the African continent, whereas the two distinct colors reflect the history of the country: This archipelago was a British colony until 1963, and in 1964 Zanzibar and the mainland territory of Tanganyika joined to form the United Republic of Tanzania. To seal this union, the Tanzanian flag adopted the colors of the two former states.

Continent: Africa
Capital: Dodoma
Currency: Tanzanian shilling
Official languages: Swahili, English
Area: 364,901 sq. mi.
Highest point: Mount Kilimanjaro (19,340 ft.)

This funny-looking monkey is only found on the island of Zanzibar, hence its name, the Zanzibar colobus.

UGANDA
Capital: Kampala

For its flag, the country of Uganda decided to sing the praises of nature, which has a special place in the hearts of all the citizens. A national symbol, the gray-crowned crane stands on one foot, facing the flag's mast. This splendid wading bird is protected by Ugandan law.

ZIMBABWE
Capital: Harare

The golden bird of Zimbabwe is a national star! It appears on the country's currency (bills and coins), as well. Propped up proudly on its pedestal, the bird is a reproduction of a primitive statue found in the ruins of an ancient city. A national treasure, the bird evokes the cultural roots of this southeastern African country, bordering Mozambique and South Africa.

ERITREA

Eritrea placed an olive branch, a symbol of peace, on its national flag. It withstood thirty years of war against its Ethiopian neighbor, represented by thirty leaves of the olive branch. Yet today, the country is still faced with frequent conflicts.

In fact, in this desert region called the "Horn of Africa," the position of Eritrea, which strategically borders the sea, aroused great envy. Did you know that Eritrea got its name from a Greek word meaning "red," due to its proximity to the Red Sea?

Continent: Africa
Capital: Asmara
Currency: nakfa
Official languages: Tigre, Arabic
Area: 46,774 sq. mi.
Highest point: Mount Soira (9,885 ft.)

Eritrea boasts 600 miles of coastline along the Red Sea! Traditional fishing plays an important role in the country's economy.

118

NIGER

The sun shines brightly over Niger, but it also radiates out from its flag! Situated in one of the hottest and sunniest regions of the planet, Niger decided to pay homage to the sun by placing it in the center of its flag.

As for the tricolored stripes, the orange stripe reminds us that Niger is among the driest countries of the planet. The Ténéré Desert is a vast swath of terrain in the country, 950 miles long by 375 miles wide!

The Niger River, which crosses almost 350 miles of the country, is represented by the white stripe. And the green stripe stands for the rare fertile zones along the riverbanks.

Continent: Africa
Capital: Niamey
Currency: West African CFA franc
Official language: French
Area: 459,286 sq. mi.
Highest point: Mont Bagzane (6,634 ft.)

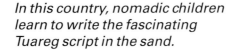

In this country, nomadic children learn to write the fascinating Tuareg script in the sand.

NAMIBIA
Capital: Windhoek

The sandy Kalahari Desert extends from Namibia to South Africa and crosses through Botswana, over an area of 360,000 square miles. It is hot—very hot—in the desert, and Namibia chose to feature a beautiful sun on its flag, symbolizing life and energy. The diagonal stripes refer to the colors of the Ovambos, the largest ethnic group in the country.

BOTSWANA
Capital: Gaborone

The light blue stripes found on the flag of Botswana refer to the abundant rain that fertilizes the soil and irrigates the Okavango River, a reservoir of water essential to the survival of the inhabitants of this arid country. The colors white and black symbolize racial equality, though it has also been said that the colors may refer to the many zebras that call Botswana home.

CAPE VERDE

Did you know that Cape Verde, situated in the middle of the Atlantic Ocean, is a volcanic archipelago composed of ten principal islands? That explains the ten stars that appear on the nation's flag. They are organized in a circle to symbolize unity—the ultramarine blue of the Atlantic Ocean blending into the sky in the horizon.

The islands were uninhabited when the Portuguese landed on them in 1456. Slave ships began making stops on the islands to transport thousands of African slaves to America—a dark chapter in the islands' history. Cape Verdeans added the color white to the flag, symbolizing peace, as well as a red stripe, representing the future and progress.

Nowadays amateur European sailors make a stopover here on their journeys across the Atlantic Ocean.

Continent: Africa
Capital: Praia
Currency: escudo
Official language: Portuguese
Area: 1,557 sq. mi.
Highest point: Mount Fogo (9,281 ft.)

The singer Cesaria Evora helped raise the profile of Cape Verde in the world.

RWANDA

Notice the radiant sunshine emanating from Rwanda's flag—a symbol of unity among Rwanda's diverse ethnicities (Hutus, Tutsis, and Twa). The sun and its rays illuminate the Rwandan people.

However, it wasn't always like this: In 1994 the Rwandan genocide (the mass killing of people based on ethnicity) led to the deaths of millions of people in just a few short months. Today, Rwanda is trying to rebuild itself around the principles represented in its tricolored flag.

The color green symbolizes the natural resources of the country, as well as the hope for prosperity through the strength and resolve of the Rwandan people. The color yellow symbolizes success. The color blue symbolizes happiness and the renewal of peace.

Continent: Africa
Capital: Kigali
Currency: Rwandan franc
Official languages: Kinyarwanda, French, English
Area: 10,185 sq. mi.
Highest point: Mount Karisimbi (14,787 ft.)

Inhabitants fleeing Rwanda during the war in 1994.

MOZAMBIQUE

Mozambique is a country with a sad history: After five centuries of Portuguese colonization, the country was ravaged by civil war for sixteen years, from 1976 to 1992, resulting in nearly a million deaths and provoking an exodus of three million people.

Such is the reason behind the aggressive colors and blunt symbols of the country's national flag. The colors green, yellow, and red underscore Mozambique's pride of belonging to the African continent. But what do the assault rifle, hoe, and open book signify? They are symbols of armed conflict, agricultural labor, and study, respectively—three values defended by the current government of Mozambique.

Today the opposition wants to remove the image of the assault rifle from the flag, in order to give a more positive image of the country.

Continent: Africa
Capital: Maputo
Currency: metical
Official language: Portuguese
Area: 308,642 sq. mi.
Highest point: Mount Binga (7,992 ft.)

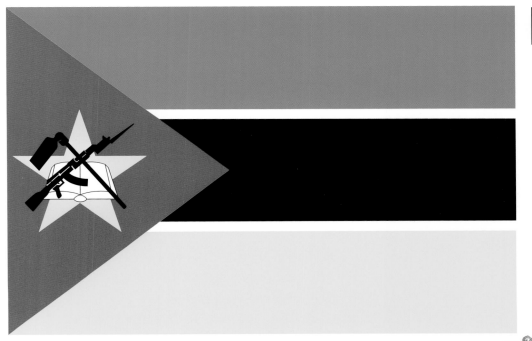

Children from Mozambique play awale, *a game made from a hollowed-out piece of wood, which uses seeds as pawns.*

LIBYA

Continent: Africa
Capital: Tripoli
Currency: Libyan dinar
Official language: Arabic
Area: 679,362 sq. mi.
Highest point: Picco Bette (7,500 ft.)

In 2011, after the fall of Colonel Muammar Gaddafi's forty-year regime, the Colonel's all-green flag was replaced with the banner of the ancient Kingdom of Libya, revived by the rebels during a very bloody war. In 1951, that flag crowned the country independent from the Italian colonization that had lasted for three decades.

On the new flag, the fertile half-moon and the star symbol of Idris, the first king of Libya, stand out over red, black and green stripes, which symbolize, respectively, the three traditional provinces of Fezzan, Cyrenaica, and Tripolitania.

On July 7, 2012, after a period of political instability, the country opened its ballot boxes for its first free elections in history.

In Libya, where 90 percent of the country is covered in rocks and sand, oases are essential to agriculture.

SEYCHELLES

As you can see, the flag of Seychelles is the opposite of Libya's: It is marked by a wide-ranging and unique assortment of colors! The white-sanded beaches and clear, blue waters of these islands partly inspired the national flag. The multicolored stripes evoke its postcard-perfect landscapes. The Indian Ocean and the limitless sky are denoted by the color blue. The verdant nature of this archipelago (composed of nearly ninety-two islands and islets) is represented by the color green. This is rounded out by red, which symbolizes the unity of the people, and white, which signifies justice.

Continent: Africa
Capital: Victoria
Currency: Seychelles rupee
Official languages: Creole, French, English
Area: 176 sq. mi.
Highest point: Morne Seychellois (2,969 ft.)

Coconuts are the largest seeds in the world.

127

CENTRAL AFRICAN REPUBLIC

This national flag, marked by a red stripe down its center, perfectly illustrates the name of this country, the Central African Republic, located in the heart of the African continent. This is one of the most colorful flags in Africa. But where does the choice of colors come from?

The Central African Republic's flag mixes together the colors of the French flag (blue, white, and red), in memory of its former colonizer, and the traditional colors of Africa (red, yellow, and green), as a gesture of fraternity and pride.

As for the five-pointed star, it appears as a symbol of unity and understanding between peoples who have endured conflicts in the past.

Continent: Africa
Capital: Bangui
Currency: Central African CFA franc
Official languages: Sango, French
Area: 240,324
Highest point: Mount Ngaoui (4,625 ft.)

Pygmies are nomadic people from the Central African Republic, the Democratic Republic of Congo, Gabon, and Cameroon.

KENYA

Kenya's flag is easy to recognize! It features the spears and shield of the Maasai people, the most well-known warriors and cattle breeders in Kenya. These weapons show the Kenyans are prepared to defend their freedom.

But why did they choose the Maasai people when there are more than seventy different ethnic groups in Kenya? Simply put, it is to pay homage to their courage: The Maasai people resisted the Kenyan government's attempts to make them adopt a more modern, and therefore sedentary, lifestyle. Their resistance showed how linked they were with nature.

Did you know that the word Kenya in the Kinkuyu language means "Mountain of Brightness," which refers to the name of the highest point in the country, Mount Kenya, standing at 17, 058 feet?

Continent: Africa
Capital: Nairobi
Currency: Kenyan shilling
Official languages: English, Swahili
Area: 224,961 sq. mi.
Highest point: Mount Kenya (17,058 ft.)

The Maasai people are cattle breeders. There is a saying in Kenya: "A man without a herd is not a man."

LESOTHO

Lesotho was founded in the nineteenth century by King Moshoeshoe I, as a way of bringing together the various ethnicities that were fleeing the Zulu invasions.

A neutral, easily identifiable symbol was needed to unify these diverse groups. A traditional Basotho hat was ultimately chosen, and it is still worn today by the inhabitants of this mountainous kingdom. This small country, round as button, is situated inside South Africa. In the country's high plateaus, rain falls in abundance, fertilizing the soil and replenishing the country's many reservoirs. The blue and green stripes in the flag are there to remind us of that fact and perfectly illustrate the country's motto: "Peace, Rain, Prosperity."

Continent: Africa
Capital: Maseru
Currency: loti
Official languages: Sotho, English
Area: 11,720 sq. mi.
Highest Point: Thabana Ntlenyana (11,424 ft.)

This is the traditional Basotho hat whose silhouette appears on the flag.

MALAWI

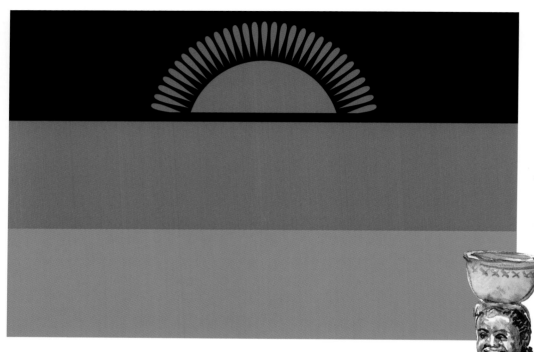

The sun rises over the horizon on the flag of Malawi.

As a matter of fact, the word *Malawi* evokes the glitter of the sun rising across the lake of the same name. The thirty-one rays of sun against the flag's black background mark the fact that Malawi was the thirty-first African state to declare its independence, an independence that was painstakingly acquired, as signified by the flag's red stripe, a symbol of strength and courage.

The color green was chosen to portray this country that is made up of highlands that extend 373 miles along Malawi Lake (the third-largest lake in Africa). Green evokes the fertility of the fields, with its great tobacco and tea plantations, as well as the country's lush vegetation.

Continent: Africa
Capital: Lilongwe
Currency: kwacha
Official language: Chichewa
Area: 45,747 sq. mi.
Highest Point: Mount Mlanje (9,849 ft.)

Malawi Lake is one of the largest in Africa. Nevertheless, natives must still fetch water from wells!

132

DEMOCRATIC
REPUBLIC OF CONGO

In February 2006 on the streets of Kinshasa, Congo's capital, enthusiastic crowds sang and danced to the rhythm of drums, celebrating a new government and a brand-new flag!

Joseph Kabila, the youngest head of state in the world, was only thirty years old in 2001 when he succeeded his dictator father. He decided to adopt a new flag as a message of peace and unity among the country's diverse ethnicities. The star, as golden as the sun, symbolizes this unity. Joseph Kabila also wanted to show his promise of peace for the country, as represented by the flag's sky blue color.

Continent: Africa
Capital: Kinshasa
Currency: Congolese franc
Official language: French
Area: 905,355 sq. mi.
Highest Point: Margherita Peak (16,795 ft.)

The fascinating Bonobo apes are the closest relatives to humans. Cuddling is among their habits.

SOUTH AFRICA

The flag of South Africa has a diverse range of colors laid out in harmony. Yet throughout the country's history, harmony has not always been so strong.

From 1948 to 1991, South Africa was marked by four distinct ethnic groups (whites, people of mixed race, Bantus, and Indians), and the mixed-race, Bantu, and Indian populations did not have the same rights as white South Africans. This type of segregation is called apartheid.

The first multiracial elections, held in 1994, marked the end of apartheid. On that day, Zulus and Afrikaners alike were finally able to vote!

A new, multicolored flag was adopted to mark this historic occasion. The different colors selected were from previous flags. The horizontal *Y* shape is a symbol of the victory of unity of all the country's diverse ethnic groups.

Continent: Africa
Capital: Pretoria
Currency: rand
Official languages: Afrikaans, English, Ndebele, Pedi, Sotho, Swazi, Tsonga, Tswana, Venda, Xhosa, Zulu
Area: 471,011 sq. mi.
Highest Point: Njesuthi Mountain (11,181 ft.)

Nelson Mandela, a Nobel Peace Prize winner, spent over twenty-five years in prison before his country achieved democracy.

MADAGASCAR

This country is famously the home of lemurs (small, primitive, tree-dwelling primates). Situated in the middle of the Indian Ocean, it is the fourth-largest island in the world. Its flag is quite simple. There is no symbol or star to speak of. The people preferred to pay tribute to the Malagasy people on its national flag. They are represented by three rectangles: The red and white stand for the majority Hova ethnic group, while green stands for all the remaining ethnic minorities on the island, especially those that live along the coasts.

Yet these colors have another significance. The color ochre refers to laterite, a reddish claylike material that covers the ground; white is the color of rice, one of Madagascar's primary crops; and green is a reference to the ravinala, "the traveler's tree," an emblem of Madagascar and a symbol of unity between humans and nature.

Continent: Africa
Capital: Antananarivo
Currency: ariary
Official languages: Malagasy, French, English
Area: 226,662 sq. mi.
Highest Point: Mount Maromokotro (9,446 ft.)

Madagascar's flora and fauna, such as lemurs, are among the most fascinating and unique in the world.

ANGOLA

The colors and symbols on Angola's flag definitely leave an impression! The machete, a broad, heavy knife, evokes the country's peasantry; it is used to cut down sugar cane. As for the cogwheel, it is a symbol of the working class.

Why do these two distinct symbols appear on the national flag? Because these two classes provide Angola with its essential economic resources. The color yellow evokes the richness of the country's soil: It is said that the abundance of copper, oil, diamonds, and gold would make Angola the richest country in Africa, if it was not weakened by frequent armed conflicts.

Continent: Africa
Capital: Luanda
Currency: kwanza
Official language: Portuguese
Area: 481,354 sq. mi.
Highest Point: Morro de Moco (8,596 ft.)

Sugar cane and coffee crops are among Angola's most important agricultural resources.

137

SOMALIA
Capital: Mogadishu

On Somalia's flag, the star evokes the unity of the Somalis, the nomadic people who make up two-thirds of the population. Many Somalis live beyond the Somalian border (in Djibouti, northeastern Kenya, the Ogaden region, and Somaliland), in the geographic zone known as the Horn of Africa.

DJIBOUTI
Capital: Djibouti

On the flag of Djibouti, a star also symbolizes unity among the country's diverse ethnic groups. The two colors represent the two majority ethnic groups in the country: Blue stands for the Issa, and green for the Afar. These two groups, who once fought against each other, showcase their desire to live in peace, despite their differences.

BURUNDI

The inhabitants of Burundi have been celebrating the sorghum harvest for hundreds of years. In their ceremonies, men sing and dance in a semicircle to the sound of the tam-tam. That's why, until 1967, Burundi's green, red, and white flag featured a tambour drum in the center. Today, the flag has three stars that illustrate the country's motto: "Unity, Work, Progress"—more serious values, even if dance still plays an important role in the country. It is said that the three stars also represent the country's three ethnic groups: the Tutsi, Hutu, and Twa, who fought each other for a long time, resulting in thousands of deaths. Fortunately, a peace accord was signed in June 2003.

Continent: Africa
Capital: Bujumbura
Currency: Burundi franc
Official languages: French, Kirundi
Area: 10,740 sq. mi.
Highest Point: Mount Heha (9,055 ft.)

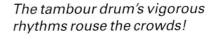

The tambour drum's vigorous rhythms rouse the crowds!

139

LIBERIA

Have you noticed the nod to the United States on the flag of Liberia? Americans founded this country in Africa.

Let's revisit a bit of history: The United States abolished the slave trade in 1807, meaning that it was no longer allowed to bring slaves to American soil. An American association had the idea to create a nation where liberated slaves could return to the land of their ancestors on the African continent. In the span of one century, twenty-two thousand liberated slaves landed in this country of lagoons and mangroves, which was named "Liberia," as in the word *liberate*, to celebrate the freedom of its inhabitants.

Unfortunately, this country is currently ravaged by all kinds of armed conflict, making it one of the most dangerous countries in Africa.

Continent: Africa
Capital: Monrovia
Currency: Liberian dollar
Official language: English
Area: 37,743 sq. mi.
Highest Point: Mount Wuteve (4,528 ft.)

Former slaves land on the shores of Liberia.

ASIA

143

TURKEY

Happiness, health, and fertility are the promises represented on the Turkish flag, bathed in the light of the crescent moon and star. Did you know that these are both symbols of Islam, much like the cross is a symbol of Christianity? In fact 99 percent of the Turkish population is Muslim. Turkey is the first country to have adorned its flag with a crescent moon. Many others have followed suit, including Uzbekistan, Turkmenistan, and Azerbaijan.

Continent: Asia
Capital: Ankara
Currency: Turkish lira
Official language: Turkish
Area: 302,535 sq. mi.
Highest point: Mount Ararat (16,949 ft.)

The Hagia Sophia church in Istanbul was converted into a mosque by Turks in the fifteenth century.

144

ISRAEL

History and religion come together on the Israeli flag! The blue star, called the Star of David, represents the Jewish people. This Magen David, or "Shield of David," was once used as a talisman by Hebrew kings. During the Second World War, it was worn in a discriminatory way to distinguish Jews (the "yellow star").

This star indicates the four cardinal points, with heaven symbolized by the top point and earth by the bottom.

The white and blue colors on the flag are a direct reference to the *tallit*, the Jewish prayer shawl. Created in the nineteenth century, the Israeli flag was officially adopted in May 1948, when Israel was established.

Continent: Asia
Capital: Jerusalem
Currency: sheqel
Official languages: Hebrew, Arabic
Area: 8,357 sq. mi.
Highest point: Mount Hermon (7,336 ft.)

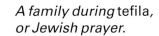

A family during tefila, *or Jewish prayer.*

UZBEKISTAN

Have you ever heard of the Uzbek emir Tamerlane (whose name means "iron" in Turco-Mongol)? A formidable warrior, in the fourteenth century he built an immense empire in Uzbekistan, founded on force and tyranny. The Uzbek flag has preserved traces of it: Six centuries later, the blue of Tamerlane still flies on the national flag.

What do you think the crescent moon and twinkling stars represent on the top part of the flag? The crescent symbolizes the fact that more than 70 percent of the population is Muslim, as does green, the color of Islam. The twelve stars stand for the twelve months of the astronomical calendar, which regulates the lives of Uzbeks, the majority of whom are cotton farmers.

Continent: Asia
Capital: Tashkent
Currency: sum
Official language: Uzbek
Area: 172,700 sq. mi.
Highest point: Adelunga Toghi
(14,111 ft.)

During the season of the cotton harvest, everyone toils in the fields for more than two months.

AZERBAIJAN

The flag of Azerbaijan depicts important aspects of the country. The eight-pointed star in the center corresponds to the eight different ethnic groups that make up the country (principally Azeris, Yakuts, Tatars, Kazakhs, and Kipchaks). Do the crescent moon and the color green ring a bell?

That's right! They are the symbols of Islam, the religion of Azerbaijan.

What about the color red—what characteristic of the country does it represent? It represents the hope for modernization and progress. It also symbolizes freedom.

Continent: Asia
Capital: Baku
Currency: manat
Official language: Azerbaijani
Area: 33,409 sq. mi.
Highest point: Bazardyuzu Dagi (14,652 ft.)

Festivals, Independence Day, or New Year's—anytime is a good time for playing music.

MALDIVES Capital: Male

The crescent moon, a symbol of the Islamic religion, appears on these four flags.

Of these countries, only Singapore is not predominantly Islamic. Mosques, Gothic cathedrals, Hindu divinity figures, Chinese pagodas, and Buddhist temples can all be found in this island nation.

In Singapore's case, the crescent moon symbolizes the nation's expansion and development. The five stars next to it represent democracy, peace, progress, justice, and equality.

PAKISTAN Capital: Islamabad

MALAYSIA Capital: Kuala Lumpur

SINGAPORE Capital: Singapore

TURKMENISTAN

Among the flags showcasing tradition, Turkmenistan's is an excellent example. On the left-hand side appear the intricate designs of handmade Turkmen carpets. They are a symbol of the traditional lives of nomads in this Central Asian region bordering the Caspian Sea.

The color green that makes up the rest of the flag is the color of the Tatar people as well as that of Islam, which is represented by the crescent moon. The moon also symbolizes hope for a shining future.

Serenity and generosity are represented by five stars, which also stand for the five senses: hearing, touch, sight, smell, and taste. Once again, the moon and stars have fascinating significance!

Continent: Asia
Capital: Ashgabat
Currency: manat
Official language: Turkmen
Area: 188,500 sq. mi.
Highest point: Gora Ayribaba (10,299 ft.)

Carpet-weaving requires hours of work. It represents the pride and prosperity of nomadic Turkmen.

150

KYRGYZSTAN

Did you know that in the Kyrgyz language the word for red is . . . *kyrgyz*? No wonder the Kyrgyz flag pays homage to this shade and has adopted red as its national color!

Inside the sun in the center of the flag is a ringlike symbol containing six intersecting arches. Do you know what they represent? The crown of a yurt, a traditional, collapsible tentlike dwelling. In these far-flung, often hostile lands where the climate can be harsh, the Kyrgyz people must be able to easily dismantle their mobile homes and stake out new, milder pastures, with herds in tow.

Continent: Asia
Capital: Bishkek
Currency: som
Official languages: Kyrgyz, Russian
Area: 76,641 sq. mi.
Highest point: Pik Pobedy (24,406 ft.)

This small country is the least developed of Central Asia. The yurt is an ideal way of living closer to nature.

KAZAKHSTHAN

Blue as far as the eye can see! And for good reason: Imagine the sun setting over Kazakhstan's ancient Mongol Empire—a 1,240-mile stretch between the Caspian Sea to the west and the Altai Mountains to the east. Khazakhstan is the largest country in Central Asia. The color blue takes pride of place on the country's flag, symbolizing well-being and tranquility.

The golden sun shining in the flag's sky evokes the wealth of the country, with its gold and oil reserves. And the majestic bird in the sky? A steppe eagle in full flight. Traditionally, the Kazakh people are experts at training eagles, used to hunt hares, marmots, and even wolves.

Continent: Asia
Capital: Astana
Currency: tenge
Official languages: Kazakh, Russian
Area: 1,052,090 sq. mi.
Highest point: Pik Khan-Tengri (22,949 ft.)

A Kazakh trainer and his steppe eagle.

MONGOLIA

Mongolia's national flag stands out for the design featured on the left-hand side. It is basically a totem, a kind of sculpture that represents the ideals of the Mongolian people. At the top, fire represents renewal and the family hearth. The three flames evoke the past, present, and future of Mongolia. The circle, be it the sun or the moon, is a reference to the religion of the Mongols—Buddhism. The opposing forces of nature are represented by the symbol of the yin and the yang, signs of wisdom and vigilance. The death of the enemy is announced by way of arrows pointing downward. Justice and honesty are represented by the two horizontal rectangles. As for the two vertical rectangles, they symbolize the friendship that unifies the country, whose proverb is: "Two friends are stronger than stone."

Continent: Asia
Capital: Ulan Bator
Currency: tugrik
Official language: Mongolian
Area: 603,909 sq. mi.
Highest point: Nayramadlin Orgil (14,350 ft.)

In this country of vast plains, livestock is classified into two groups: those with "cool" muzzles and those with "warm" muzzles.

TAJIKISTAN

"Heaven is composed of seven beautiful orchards, separated by seven mountains, each with a shining star on top . . ." That is the origin of the seven stars poised above the golden crown, Tajikistan's coat of arms. Did you know that Tajikistan's Pamir mountain chain is called the "Rooftop of the World"? These mountains are among the world's highest peaks and are covered by snow year-round, as represented by the flag's central white stripe. The color white also evokes the cotton crop, an essential export of this Central Asian country. The green stripe symbolizes the rare valleys in this mountainous country, but it is also the color of Islam, Tajikistan's official religion.

Continent: Asia
Capital: Dushanbe
Currency: somoni
Official language: Tajik
Area: 55,300 sq. mi.
Highest point: Qullai Ismoili Somoni (24,590 ft.)

In many regions in Tajikistan, wheat is harvested by hand and then loaded onto trucks.

GEORGIA

Georgia's five-cross flag was officially adopted in 2004, but it had already been flown by Georgian lords since the Middle Ages. Saint George's Cross, which cuts the flag into four parts, symbolizes the martyrdom of Saint George, a Christian tortured to death in the fourth century by the Roman emperor Diocletian. His legend grew during the course of the centuries, and in the Middle Ages he was very popular among crusaders in the Holy Lands. In fact, the four smaller red crosses on the flag represent these knights.

Continent: Asia
Capital: Tblisi
Currency: lari
Official language: Georgian
Area: 27,086 sq. mi.
Highest point: Mount Shkhara (16,627 ft.)

According to Greek mythology, it was in Georgia that the Argonauts went searching for the Golden Fleece of the winged ram, an antique, bejeweled treasure.

156

ARMENIA

Red, blue, and orange. Do you recognize this tricolored flag? The colors of the Armenian flag have varying significance. It has often been said that red symbolizes the blood shed by the Armenians while defending their country against the Turks during World War I.

Orange represents the fertile lands of this country known for its vineyards. It has also been said that orange evokes the color of apricots, a fruit crop grown in vast quantities in the country, while also paying tribute to the hard labor of workers who toil in the fields. Others say that orange corresponds to the courage of Armenians. Blue signifies the sunny, cloudless Armenian sky.

Continent: Asia
Capital: Yerevan
Currency: dram
Official language: Armenian
Surface area: 11,484 sq. mi.
Highest point: Mount Aragats
(13,418 ft.)

*Armenians practice an
Orthodox Christian faith.*

157

SAUDI ARABIA

Do you speak Arabic? If so, you'll have no problem reading (from right to left, of course) this phrase called the *Shahadah*, the Islamic declaration of faith: "There is no God but Allah, and Muhammad is his Messenger."

Faith in Allah is thus represented on the Saudi flag.

The drawn sword symbolizes the fact that in this country, the largest of the Arab peninsula, one is ready to fight for Allah. Other countries, such as Afghanistan, Iran, Iraq, and Brunei, have also used writing on their flags to showcase their beliefs, opinions, or commandments.

Continent: Asia
Capital: Riyadh
Currency: Riyal
Official language: Arabic
Area: 830,000 sq. mi.
Highest point: Jabal Sawda (10,213 ft.)

Saudi Arabia is in possession of the largest oil and gas reserves in the world.

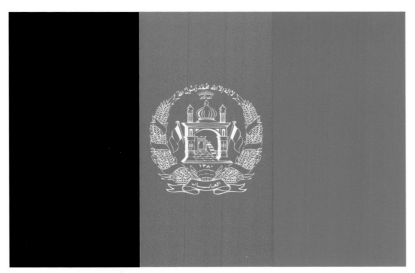

AFGHANISTAN Capital: Kabul

IRAN Capital: Tehran

BRUNEI Capital: Bandar Seri Begawan

IRAQ Capital: Baghdad

LEBANON

Cedar, the "most famous natural monument," appears in the center of the Lebanese flag and is a traditional symbol of the country. *Arz el-Rab* is Arabic for the "cedar of God," reflecting the importance of the tree to the country's Muslims and Christians: Christians consider the cedar a holy tree, and Muslims believe its wood is pure. Cedar is found in the country's temples, churches, and mosques and symbolizes strength, eternity (since it can live for hundreds of years), holiness, and peace. That is quite a meaningful symbol for a country that has experienced its share of armed conflict. As a matter of fact, the red stripes evoke all the sacrifices made in the struggle for independence.

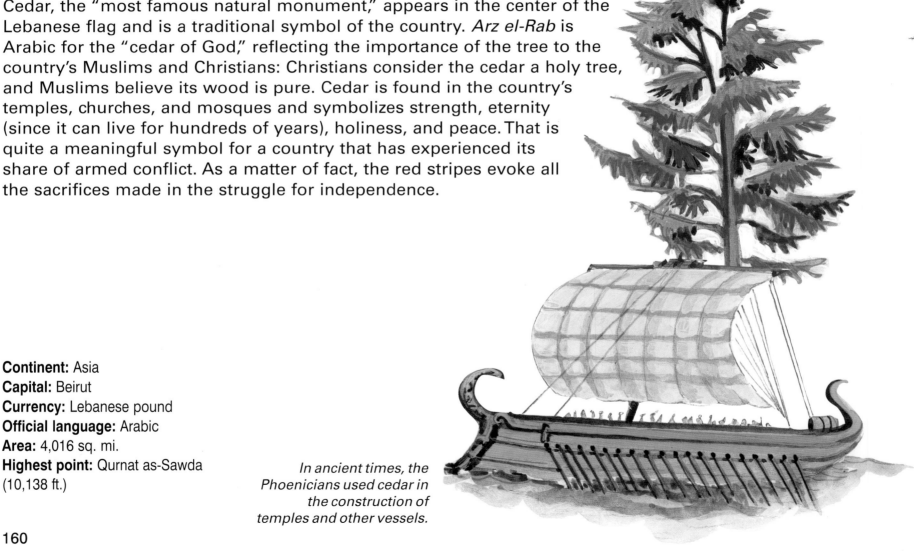

Continent: Asia
Capital: Beirut
Currency: Lebanese pound
Official language: Arabic
Area: 4,016 sq. mi.
Highest point: Qurnat as-Sawda (10,138 ft.)

In ancient times, the Phoenicians used cedar in the construction of temples and other vessels.

160

UNITED ARAB EMIRATES

Continent: Asia
Capital: Abu Dhabi
Currency: dirham
Official language: Arabic
Area: 32,280 sq. mi.
Highest point: Jabal Yibir (5,010 ft.)

More than 150 years ago, pirates crisscrossed the Persian Gulf. Shorelines were far from safe along the "Pirate Coast." In 1853, Great Britain signed a perpetual maritime truce with these small states that are called emirates. They were regrouped under the name "Trucial States," and placed under British protection. There are seven Arab emirates. Nowadays, the coasts are safe and the country's neutrality is symbolized by the white stripe on the flag.

You will surely recognize green as the traditional color of Islam, but it also stands for the fertility of the region, while the colors red, white, and black bring to mind the Arab revolt in the beginning of the nineteenth century. Black also evokes oil, which in this country flows freely.

Until the nineteenth century, it wasn't easy to wander along the Pirate Coast without getting nabbed by pirates.

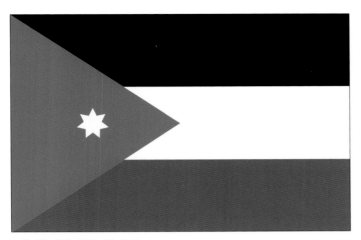

JORDAN Capital: Amman

Just like the flags of Iraq and the United Arab Emirates, these flags contain Pan-Arab colors.

They stem from the flag of the Arab revolt, which took place at the beginning of the twentieth century and whose aim was to liberate the Arab countries that were under the yoke of the Ottoman Empire.

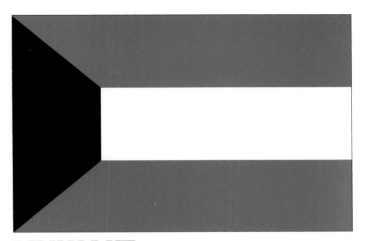

KUWAIT Capital: Kuwait

Green traditionally symbolizes Islam. The other colors evoke the various difficult periods these Arab countries were subjected to: black for periods of oppression and red for bloody battles. White stands for hope in the future. These colors are identical to those of the Arab dynasties.

YEMEN Capital: Sanaa

SYRIA Capital: Damascus

BAHRAIN

Bahrain's flag contains five sharp edges. Why? Because on February 18, 2002, the emir of Bahrain, who proclaimed himself king only several days prior, decided to pay homage to the religion of the country. Five jagged points separate the two colors of Bahrain's flag, symbolizing the five pillars of Islam: profession of faith, prayer, alms giving, fasting during Ramadan, and the pilgrimage to Mecca.

Continent: Asia
Capital: Manama
Currency: Bahraini dinar
Official language: Arabic
Area: 281 sq. mi.
Highest point: Jabal Al-Dukhan (440 ft.)

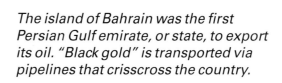

The island of Bahrain was the first Persian Gulf emirate, or state, to export its oil. "Black gold" is transported via pipelines that crisscross the country.

164

QATAR

Continent: Asia
Capital: Doha
Currency: riyal
Official language: Arabic
Area: 4,184 sq. mi.
Highest point: Qurayn Abu al Bawl (338 ft.)

Try not to confuse the flags of Qatar and Bahrain: While it is true that their resemblance is striking, a few details distinguish them from one another. First, the flag of Qatar is long—in fact it is longer than any other flag. Furthermore, its serrated band contains nine points, as opposed to Bahrain's five.

The color also varies. Long ago, Qatar used a vegetable dye that gave its flag a bright red tint. But after sun exposure, this color began to fade and eventually turned into a wine-colored red. So, this monarchy north of the Arabian Peninsula decided to definitively adopt this dark red shade for its flag.

OMAN

The Omanis have defended their territory for three centuries with swords and *gambias* (curved daggers). Reproduced on the flag, these weapons are part of the tried and tested emblems of the Sultanate of Oman. It's not surprising that the monarchy of this country, independent since the eighteenth century, depict these instruments of battle with pride on their national flag.

Oman is the easternmost country on the Arab peninsula. This is why the color red, a traditional color of Persian Gulf countries, appears on the country's flag. As for green, the color of Islam, it stands for the Jabal Akhdar (the "Green Mountains"), the country's highest peaks, and its terraced fields.

Continent: Asia
Capital: Muscat
Currency: rial
Official language: Arabic
Area: 119,500 sq. mi.
Highest point: Jabal Shams (9,777 ft.)

In this mountainous country, terraces were built in order to grow crops on flat land. This is called terrace cultivation.

166

MYANMAR

Myanmar, formerly called Burma, is ruled by the Asian monsoons. The large quantities of rice cultivated in the Irrawaddy Delta, which flows into the Indian Ocean, have earned Myanmar a reputation as the world's "rice basket."

Not long ago, Myanmar adopted new colors for its national flag, replacing the red and blue and the image of a rice stalk. The new flag has bands of yellow, green, and red. Yellow symbolizes the solidarity of the people and the sun that illuminates this Asiatic country. Green represents the fertile lands and also stands for the tranquility and peace desired by its residents. Red signifies decisiveness and the valor of the Burmese people. The large white star in the middle of the new flag evokes the hope that this Republic of the Union of Myanmar shall become a sustainable and stable country.

Continent: Asia
Capital: Rangoon
Currency: kyat
Official language: Burmese
Area: 261,228 sq. mi.
Highest point: Hkakabo Razi (19,295 ft.)

The Padaung wear rings around their necks starting from childhood.

167

CAMBODIA

Taking pride in its thousand-year history, the kingdom of Cambodia ("Kampuchea" in the Khmer language) features one of the most beautiful temples in the world on its flag—Angkor Wat. Situated in the heart of a lush jungle, the ruins of this ancient capital of the Khmer Empire, a UNESCO World Heritage Site, attracts thousands of amazed visitors each year.

The white temple of the Buddhist religion appears on a red background, representing the Cambodian people, and is bordered by two blue stripes, symbolizing the monarchy. Blue, red, and white are also the colors found on the flags of Laos and Thailand, Cambodia's neighbors.

Continent: Asia
Capital: Phnom Penh
Currency: riel
Official language: Khmer
Area: 69,898 sq. mi.
Highest point: Phnom Aôral (5,949 ft.)

Bikes are the most frequently used mode of transportation in Cambodia. They are used to get from place to place and to transport goods and animals.

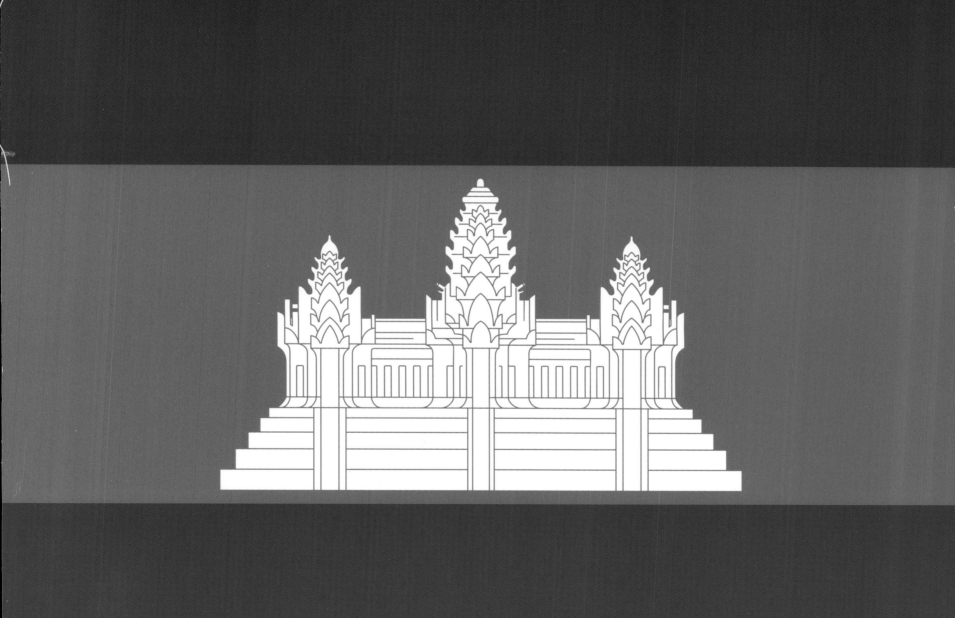

THAILAND

In "the land of the white elephant," an elephant appeared on the national flag until 1917. Do you know why it disappeared? Here's the story: A hundred years ago, the reigning dynasty adopted a white elephant as its emblem, which ultimately appeared on the national flag. One day, the king saw the flag hanging upside down from its mast, showing the elephant in a position that was anything but royal! To prevent it from happening again, he decided to remove the elephant and replace it with a symmetrical flag featuring the ancestral color of the ancient kingdom of Siam: royal blue.

It has been said that the colored stripes pay homage to the Allies of World War II—the French, British, Americans, and Russians—all of whose flags have these colors.

What a way to show solidarity!

Continent: Asia
Capital: Bangkok
Currency: baht
Official language: Thai
Area: 198,117 sq. mi.
Highest point: Doi Inthanon (8,481 ft.)

The white elephant is an extremely rare albino animal, allegedly endowed with magical powers.

170

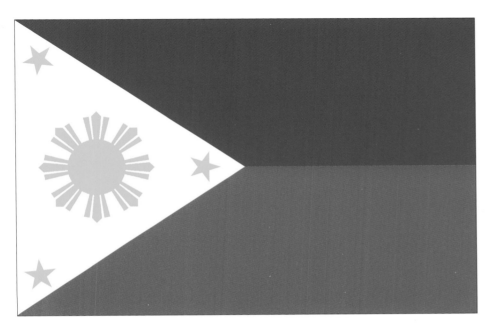

PHILIPPINES
Capital: Manila

If you ever visit the Philippines, take a good look at its national flag. The blue stripe symbolizes peace, truth, and justice, and the red stripe, patriotism and bravery. But beware if the colored stripes are inversed (the red on top and the blue on the bottom)! In the Philippines, when the colors are inversed, it means that the country is at war.

INDONESIA
Capital: Jakarta

The colored stripes of the Indonesian flag shouldn't be flipped. Otherwise, one would confuse it with the flag of Poland. You might have noticed that the Indonesian flag is an exact replica of that of Monaco—probably the only point in common between the largest archipelago in the world (spanning nearly 3,200 miles) and the tiny "rock" of Monaco.

BHUTAN

Do dragons exist? That's a difficult question to answer for anyone but the inhabitants of Bhutan! The official name of the country is Druk-Yul, which means "land of the dragon" in Dzongkha. So it's only normal that the national flag features a fire-breathing dragon.

Although this legendary animal sometimes signifies evil in Western society, in Asia it's considered lucky. The flames emanating from the dragon's mouth chase away bad spirits and symbolize the strength of this small country, sandwiched between two giants, China and India.

The pearls in the dragon's claws symbolize wealth and prosperity. Today, Bhutan is the last Buddhist kingdom in the world. And can you guess who rules it? The only "Dragon King" on the planet! Do not fear—it's only the nickname of the king, Druk Gyalpo.

Continent: Asia
Capital: Thimphu
Currency: ngultrum
Official language: Dzongkha (a Tibetan dialect)
Area: 14,824 sq. mi.
Highest point: Kula Kangri (24,780 ft.)

Images of herds of yaks hark back to ancient times.

SRI LANKA

The king of the animal kingdom brandishes a sword on the flag of Sri Lanka, giving this island nation in the Indian Ocean all of its strength. Why? Simply because the former name of Sri Lanka, Ceylon, stems from the word *sinhala*, which means "lion." Ceylon must bring to mind something else as well: tea! Sri Lanka, the name ultimately adopted for the country in 1972, means "resplendent land," after its heavenly landscapes. The island is composed of a mosaic of religions, which the Sri Lankan flag attempts to capture. Islam is represented by the color green, and Hinduism by saffron. Pipal leaves, from the sacred Buddhist tree, are placed in each corner of the crimson rectangle. They stand for kindness, friendliness, happiness, and equanimity.

Continent: Asia
Capital: Colombo
Currency: Sri Lankan rupee
Official languages: Singhala, Tamil
Area: 25,332 sq. mi.
Highest point: Pidurutalagala (8,281 ft.)

It was under a pipal tree that Siddhartha, the founder of Buddhism, attained enlightenment and became the Buddha.

INDIA

This flag looks almost exactly like that of Niger, in Africa, but the Indian flag has the distinction of having at its center a wheel called a *chakra*, an ancient Buddhist symbol. As blue as the sea and sky, it evokes the fatality of existence, as well as expressing movement, and the dynamism that motivates the Indian people.

Religion has an essential place in this immense country bordering the Indian Ocean. The colors of the flag provide a reminder: Hindus are represented by orange, the color of courage and sacrifice; and Muslims are represented by green, the color of Islam, faith, and honor.

Continent: Asia
Capital: New Delhi
Currency: Indian rupee
Official languages: Hindi, English, and twenty-one other languages
Area: 1,222,559 sq. mi.
Highest point: Kanchenjunga (28,169 ft.)

The Ganges is a sacred river for the Indians, who come here to bathe or burn the bodies of the dead.

NEPAL

The Nepali flag has the unique distinction of being the only one in the world that isn't a quadrilateral.

The two triangles symbolize the Himalayas, the highest mountain chain on the planet, where more than 110 summits exceed 24,000 feet in altitude! The triangles also evoke Buddhism and Hinduism, the country's two principal religions.

The two celestial bodies symbolize the hope that the nation will last as long as the sun and moon. The rhododendron, Nepal's national flower, is evoked by the color red, whereas the blue border is a symbol of peace.

Continent: Asia
Capital: Kathmandu
Currency: Nepali rupee
Official language: Nepali
Area: 56,827 sq. mi.
Highest point: Mount Everest
(29,028 ft.)

Deep in the Nepali mountains, multicolored prayer flags flutter in the wind.

JAPAN

In the thirteenth century, a Buddhist priest offered a sun banner to the emperor of Japan, who was considered to be a descendent of the goddess of the sun. Today, the sun goddess Amaterasu is the most venerated deity of the Shinto religion, practiced by the majority of the Japanese people. The name *Japan* actually means "source of sun."

In the beginning, the flag was once an emblem belonging to one of the largest aristocratic shogunates in the country, the Tokugawa. In 1870 it was officially adopted by the state.

In addition to evoking the sun, the red circle symbolizes passion and sincerity, whereas white stands for honesty and purity.

Continent: Asia
Capital: Tokyo
Currency: yen
Official language: Japanese
Area: 145,914 sq. mi.
Highest point: Mount Fuji (12,388 ft.)

Even though Japan stands at the pinnacle of modernity, the traditional kimono is still worn during major events.

BANGLADESH

The Bangladeshi flag features a dazzling sun. The flaming red color symbolizes the hard-earned freedom and the blood spilled by the people in the battle against Pakistan. Before 1947 India was a colony of the United Kingdom. During independence, it was split into two different states, the Indian Union (with a Hindu majority) on one side, and Pakistan (with a Muslim majority) on the other. Bangladesh, which is situated east of India, became a Pakistani province.

In Bangladesh, there are frequent monsoons, and the Ganges-Brahmaputra River delta, bordering the Indian Ocean, often floods. But the combination of this sun and rain gives the country its lush vegetation, green rice fields, and jute, of which Bangladesh is the world's leading producer.

Continent: Asia
Capital: Dhaka
Currency: taka
Official language: Bengali
Area: 56,977 sq. mi.
Highest point: Keokradong (4,035 ft.)

The sari, a wraplike dress, is common in the rice fields, where rice farmers pick the stalks and replant new seeds all day long.

179

NORTH KOREA

It was in 1948, the year of its independence, that the "Land of the Morning Calm" adopted this flag as a symbol of its new identity.

The two blue stripes represent peace, and red is a reference to socialism, the country's political doctrine. In the center, the red star is yet another reference to socialism, whereas the white circle that surrounds it represents the universe. In Chinese philosophy, the yin and yang is a symbol of perfection, infinity, and eternity; in Korean it is known as *Taeguk*.

Continent: Asia
Capital: Pyongyang
Currency: North Korean won
Official language: Korean
Area: 47,399 sq. mi.
Highest point: Paektu San (9,022 ft.)

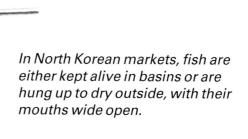

In North Korean markets, fish are either kept alive in basins or are hung up to dry outside, with their mouths wide open.

SOUTH KOREA

South Korea's flag is called the *Taegukgi*, which refers to the yin and yang symbol at its center. But what does that mean? The yin and yang are symbols of infinity, perfection, and eternity. The two big comma shapes form a complete circle. In Chinese philosophy, they represent the union of the sun in red (the yang) with night, in blue (the yin), as well as the positive and negative, and masculine and feminine. These symbols were at the origin of the "Big Bang", the moment when the universe was formed. The flag's black stripes, called trigrams, evoke the seasons, as well as air, earth, fire, and water, and much more.

Continent: Asia
Capital: Seoul
Currency: South Korean won
Official language: Korean
Area: 38,481 sq. mi.
Highest point: Halla San (6,398 ft.)

This temple was erected in honor of the great philosopher Confucius. One of his famous maxims was: "Do not impose on others what you yourself do not desire."

EAST TIMOR

The flag of East Timor flies proudly over the island of Timor, which the country shares with its giant neighbor, Indonesia. But the country has a troubled past, filled with new directions and conflicts. The large red surface of the flag stands for the people and their struggles against Portuguese colonizers, followed by Indonesian occupiers.

The yellow and black triangles correspond to the different colors of political parties that fought for the country's freedom. What is the significance of the white star, which shines in the middle of these bright colors? It guides the people toward the light, toward the future, such as the first elections, which took place in April 2001. It's a future full of promise!

Continent: Asia
Capital: Dili
Currency: U.S. dollar
Official languages: Tetum, Portuguese
Area: 5,760 sq. mi.
Highest point: Foho Tatamailau (9,721 ft.)

East Timor is located to the south of the large Indonesian archipelago, between the Sawu and Timor Seas.

LAOS

The white moon rises over the Mekong River, symbolized by the wide blue stripe. The Mekong is the country's main axis, and the primary source of crop irrigation. It is a symbol of prosperity for this nation, situated at the center of the Indo-Chinese peninsula. Before Laos became swept up in prolonged conflicts, a magnificent elephant was depicted on the national flag. In fact, the name of the country in Lao, *Lan Xang*, means a "million elephants."

The county's natural resources, such as gold, gypsum, and tin, are represented by the color red.

Continent: Asia
Capital: Vientiane
Currency: kip
Official language: Lao
Area: 91,429 sq. mi.
Highest point: Phou Bia (9,245 ft.)

In Laos, dance is a traditional art form learned in childhood. This discipline requires grace, perseverance, and patience.

CHINA

The five-starred red flag is intimately linked to the political history of this country—the most populous country in the world!

Red and yellow are traditional imperial colors, and five (the number of stars on the flag) is considered a lucky number by the Chinese. But red is also the color of the Communists, China's ruling political party for decades. The largest star on the flag is in fact a reference to the Chinese Communist Party.

The meaning of the four smaller stars isn't official, but they are thought to represent the four social classes defined by Communism (workers, peasants, the bourgeoisie, and capitalists).

Continent: Asia
Capital: Beijing
Currency: yuan
Official language: Mandarin Chinese
Area: 3,696,100 sq. mi.
Highest point: Mount Everest (29,028 ft.)

Starting in the 1950s, the government of Mao Zedong introduced mandatory uniforms for all of China's inhabitants, including children.

VIETNAM

Vietnam is one of the last four Communist countries in the world. The five-pointed yellow star on the flag is a symbol of this philosophy, as it is for other Communist countries. Just look at China's flag with the red star, North Korea's with its star in the white circle, and Cuba's.

Red represents the blood spilled by the country's inhabitants fighting for independence. For the Vietnamese people, this flag is a symbol of independence and a guide: It reminds workers, peasants, intellectuals, youth, and soldiers of their call to unity.

Continent: Asia
Capital: Hanoi
Currency: dong
Official language: Vietnamese
Area: 127,882 sq. mi.
Highest point: Fan Si Pan (10,312 ft.)

Ha Long Bay is arguably the most beautiful natural landscape in Vietnam, composed of no fewer than 1,969 islands, islets, and rocky outcrops.

INDEX

INDEX

Library of Congress Cataloging-in-Publication Data

Bednar, Sylvie.
Flags of the world / by Sylvie Bednar.
p. cm.
ISBN 978-0-8109-8010-5 (Harry N. Abrams)
1. Flags—Juvenile literature. I. Title.

CR109.B43 2009
929.9′2—dc22
2008045923

Originally published in French by Éditions de la Martinière, Paris
English translation copyright © 2009 Harry N. Abrams, Inc.
Translated by Gita Daneshjoo

Art direction and design by Christian Neveu
Cover design by Melissa Arnst

Illustrations by Christelle Guénot: Pages 14, 16, 17, 18, 22, 23, 24, 25, 26, 28, 30, 31, 36, 38, 40, 44, 46, 50, 64, 68, 72, 76, 80, 81, 88, 90, 91, 97, 100, 102, 104, 105, 108, 116, 124, 125, 128, 131, 132, 133, 134, 140, 144, 145, 146, 150, 153, 154, 155, 156, 157, 158, 162, 164, 166, 174, 175, 178, 179, 180, 181, 182, 183, 184.

Illustrations by Anne Steinlein: Pages 12, 34, 37, 42, 45, 48, 52, 54, 56, 58, 59, 60, 62, 65, 66, 70, 71, 74, 77, 82, 84, 86, 92, 94, 96, 98, 106, 112, 118, 120, 122, 126, 127, 130, 136, 137, 139, 142, 148, 152, 160, 167, 168, 170, 172, 176, 185.

Printed and bound in China
12 11 10 9 8 7 6 5

Abrams Books for Young Readers are available at special discounts when purchased in quantity for premiums and promotions as well as fundraising or educational use. Special editions can also be created to specification. For details, contact specialsales@abramsbooks.com or the address below.

THE ART OF BOOKS SINCE 1949

115 West 18th Street
New York, NY 10011
www.abramsbooks.com